On Disgust

AUREL KOLNAI

*Edited and with an
Introduction by*

Barry Smith and Carolyn Korsmeyer

OPEN COURT
Chicago and La Salle, Illinois

To order books from Open Court, call toll-free 1-800-815-2280, or visit our website at www.opencourtbooks.com.

The cover photograph is of *Ein Erzbösewicht* by Franz Xaver Messerschmidt, used by permission of the Österreichische Galerie Belvedere, Vienna.

Open Court Publishing Company is a division of Carus Publishing Company.

Library of Congress Cataloging-in-Publication Data

Kolnai, Aurel.
  [Ekel. English]
  On Disgust / Aurel Kolnai / edited and with an introduction by Barry Smith and Carolyn Korsmeyer.
    p. cm.
  Includes bibliographical references (p.   ) and index.
    ISBN 0-8126-9566-6 (pbk.)
  1. Aversion. I. Korsmeyer, Carolyn. II. Smith, Barry, Ph.D. III. Kolnai, Aurel.
  Standard modes of aversion. IV. Title.
    B1646.K7773E4413 2003
    128'.37—dc21   2003009846

Brief Contents

Detailed Contents

Preface

This volume includes two works by Aurel Kolnai. The long essay 'Disgust' is published here in English for the first time. It was written in 1927 and originally appeared in 1929 in Volume 10 of Husserl's *Jahrbuch für Philosophie und phänomenologische Forschung*. It was immediately translated into Spanish and published by Ortega y Gasset in his journal *Revista de Occidente* at the end of the same year. It was republished in German in 1974 and is still in print (Moritz Geiger / Aurel Kolnai, *Beiträge zur Phänomenologie des ästhetischen Genusses / Der Ekel* [Max Niemeyer, 1974]), and it has been translated into French (*Le dégoût*, trans. Olivier Cossé [Paris: Agalma, 1997]).

The present translation of 'Disgust' has gone through a number of stages. What follows is a thoroughly revised version of a translation prepared by Kolnai's wife Elizabeth. It also takes into account some alternate readings from an earlier translation prepared by Elisabeth Gombrich, who with her art historian brother, Ernst, was like Kolnai an emigré to England from Austria. Before her death in 1982, Elizabeth Kolnai worked further on the translation with Barry Smith and encouraged him to seek a publisher. He has again revised and retranslated portions of the essay. The editors of the present volume have endeavored to cast Kolnai's ideas into idiomatic English, while at the same time heeding the demands of the technical details of the subject-matter and the phenomenological terminology embedded in Kolnai's philosophical language.

Several years before his death in 1973, Kolnai, at the request of his London colleagues, wrote the shorter piece also printed here, 'The Standard Modes of Aversion: Fear, Hate, and Disgust'. It was published in the journal *Mind* in 1998. It's clear that Kolnai stuck by his basic assessment of these aversive emotions throughout his long philosophical career. The earlier essay is more extensive, the analysis of disgust spelled out in greater detail. The comparisons among disgust, fear, and hatred are articulated more directly and succinctly in the later piece. Together, they provide a full picture of Kolnai's insightful and original philosophical perspective on disgust.

The picture of Kolnai on page 28 was taken in Vienna about 1935, just a few years after the essay 'Disgust' was first published. The picture of Kolnai on page 92 is his identity photograph from about 1941, taken when he entered the United States. Both photographs appear in this book with the kind permission of Francis Dunlop.

We would like to thank Aurel Kolnai's literary executors, Professors David Wiggins and Bernard Williams, for their permission to publish this translation of 'Disgust'. We are especially grateful to Francis Dunlop for his advice about Kolnai's life and work. And we would like to express appreciation to Andrew Spear for preparing the index for this book. We also thank Suzanne Cunningham, Laurent Stern, Francesca Murphy, Kevin Mulligan, Andrew Cunningham, Tony Moulesong, and Eileen McNamara. Kolnai's essay, 'The Standard Modes of Aversion', is reprinted from *Mind* with the permission of Oxford University Press.

Visceral Values:
Aurel Kolnai on Disgust

CAROLYN KORSMEYER and BARRY SMITH

Disgust is a powerful, visceral emotion. It is rooted so deeply in bodily responses that some theorists have hesitated even to classify it as an emotion in the fullest sense, considering it more akin to involuntary reactions such as nausea, retching, and the startle recoil. Like these it is an aversive response and belongs among the body's protective mechanisms. Disgust helps to ensure the safety of the organism by inhibiting contact with what is foul, toxic, and thereby dangerous. But for all of its engagement of bodily responses, disgust is also an emotion that is at work in creating and sustaining our social and cultural reality. It helps us to grasp hierarchies of value, to cope with morally sensitive situations, and to discern and maintain cultural order. So strong is the revulsion of disgust that the emotion itself can appear to justify moral condemnation of its object—inasmuch as the tendency of an object to arouse disgust may seem adequate grounds to revile it. At the same time, the fact that the emotion is quick and reactive may serve to cancel out these grounds by inducing one to reflect on the reasons why disgust is aroused. Thus the experience of disgust both grounds moral perspectives and casts doubt upon their validity. It is therefore by no means a simple, visceral reaction whose cause is obvious and whose meaning is transparent.

In certain respects, disgust appears to be one of the more natural emotive responses. It is one of several basic emotions whose characteristic displays, for example facial expression and gesture, are invariant across cultures.[1] The objects that trigger disgust also have a fairly constant range: things that are decaying and putrefying, that are contaminated and contaminating, and are thus associated with

1

impurity and threat—such as corpses; open wounds; crawling, pullulating maggots. Yet the specific triggers for disgust also obviously vary from place to place. The realm of the edible, above all, provides clear examples of objects that can appear disgusting; but differences among food preferences and criteria for edibility that obtain across the globe, and even in the same individual at different times, furnish evidence for the flexibility of both taste and disgust. What is considered disgusting at one dining table is regarded as delicious at another. Thus, whatever the reactive, somatic components that figure in disgust, it is an emotion with a highly complex psychology and one that cannot be classed as simply a mechanism that provides quick protection against the dangers that flow from ingesting toxins. It is in fact a highly cognitive emotion, which provides information about features of the outer world not readily available by other means, and which also reveals something about the complexities and shadows of our inner psychic life.

Here at the start of the twenty-first century, philosophical discussions of disgust are on the increase. The revival of interest in emotions and their contribution to moral understanding represented in the works of thinkers such as Robert Solomon, Martha Nussbaum, Lawrence Blum, Patricia Greenspan, Bernard Williams, and Virginia Held has led to serious treatment of a subject that once was barely a bump on the philosophical horizon. In 1929 when Aurel Kolnai published his essay 'Der Ekel' in Edmund Husserl's *Jahrbuch für Philosophie und phänomenologische Forschung*, the house journal of the phenomenological movement, he could truly assert that disgust was a "sorely neglected" topic. (The Bibliographical Note that appears at the end of Kolnai's essay indicates how scant were the resources from which he could draw, although Kolnai's survey of relevant literature appears to have been more impressionistic than systematic.)[2] Forty years later his shorter piece on 'The Standard Modes of Aversion: Fear, Disgust, and Hatred' still predated much philosophical attention to this emotion, which remains among the least scrutinized of mental phenomena.[3] Now, however, this situation appears to be changing as philosophers, psychologists, and historians of culture are turning their attention not only to emotions in general but more specifically to the large and disturbing set of aversive emotions, including disgust and its kin: fear, contempt, horror, loathing.

Kolnai's essay appears remarkably prescient against the background of this newer scholarship. Indeed, the analysis he undertook virtually alone in the 1920s sustains comparison with such recent works as William Ian Miller's comprehensive *Anatomy of Disgust*, and also with aesthetic analyses of the emotional components of horror aroused by film and literature such as are offered by Noël Carroll, Cynthia Freeland, or Julia Kristeva.[4] Most importantly, Kolnai's work supplements the burgeoning philosophical and psychological studies of emotion with his vivid treatment of the specifics of aversion. His own approach grows out of his background in phenomenology and is methodologically closest to the work of such philosophers as Husserl and Meinong. Like the latter two Kolnai writes in a complex style that is occasionally difficult to penetrate. On the other hand, his detailed conceptual analysis is not weighed down by any general system, and it sits well with the methods of the analytic philosophers with whom Kolnai made his home in his later years. What is more, Kolnai is sensitive to the attraction as well as to the repulsion of disgust, and his insights dovetail with some of the observations of psychoanalysis. The first of Kolnai's books, *Psychoanalysis and Sociology*,[5] published when he was only twenty, was in fact a study of the social and political applications of Freud's ideas, and Kolnai was himself a member of the International Psychological Association. He abandoned psychoanalysis in 1925, shortly before writing 'Der Ekel'.

Psychoanalysis is of course one of the few schools of thought that never neglected the phenomenon of disgust. Kolnai's work thus spans a bridge not only between phenomenology and analytic philosophy but also between the philosophical and the psychological study of emotions, and for this reason, as well as for the intrinsic interest of his ideas, Kolnai's 'Disgust' repays close reading today.

Kolnai's Life

Aurel Kolnai was born in 1900 in Budapest, then still one of the capital cities of the Austro-Hungarian Empire. He was born Aurel Stein into a liberal, secular Jewish family; but he changed his surname to Kolnai in 1918, perhaps because, in the new, territorially truncated Hungarian state, being a Jew could mean becoming an ideological (even if not yet a physical) target. In 1920 Kolnai moved to Vienna, where, supplemented by funds from his father, he scratched a living as free-lance writer and editor. Two years later, he enrolled as a student of philosophy at the University of Vienna, where his teachers included Heinrich Gomperz, Moritz Schlick, Felix Kaufmann, Karl Bühler, and Ludwig von Mises. Eventually he became drawn to the thinking of Franz Brentano and to the phenomenology of Brentano's student Edmund Husserl, and for a brief period in the summer of 1928 he studied under Husserl in Freiburg.

Kolnai paid particular attention to the ideas of the so-called Munich school of realist phenomenologists, and especially to the work of Max Scheler, the most prominent figure in the Munich school, whom Kolnai first read in 1924. Kolnai was early drawn to Christianity, and Scheler's Catholicism seems to have strengthened his interest in the Catholic religion, as did the works of the English writer G. K. Chesterton. Kolnai was received into the Catholic Church in 1926 on the very day that he graduated from the University of Vienna.[6] Probably the most influential product of his Vienna years was his book *The War Against the West*, an extensive and passionate commentary criticizing the philosophical and ideological writings of National Socialism, written by Kolnai in the cafés of Vienna's Nazi underground, where literature otherwise subject to censorship was readily available.[7]

Kolnai remained in Vienna until 1937. He then lived from time to time in Paris, increasingly mindful of the threats posed by the expansion of the Hitler Reich. Shortly after his marriage to his wife, Elizabeth, in 1940, the two fled through Spain and Portugal, finally managing to emigrate first to the United States and then to Canada, where Aurel obtained his first position teaching philosophy, at the Université de Laval in Québec City. Ten years later Kolnai reached England, where he held a part-time position as 'Visiting Lecturer' at Bedford College in the University of London. Kolnai's later writings display an interesting combination of English common-sense philosophy in the style of G.E. Moore with the type of painstaking philosophical description developed by the Munich realist phenomenologists. Kolnai was throughout his life skeptical of philosophical Grand Systems in the style of Hegel or Marx in a way that reveals not only his Anglophile, Catholic background but also his roots in Austrian, not German, thinking.[8]

Kolnai's Intellectual Context

In his general approach to emotions and their objects, Kolnai follows a phenomenological method that focuses on the mode of intentionality at work in different types of experiences and the nature of objects thereby revealed. Intentionality is mental directedness towards an object, whether it be real or imaginary, that thereby becomes an 'intentional object'. (For those readers unfamiliar with the philosophical use of this term, it is important not to confuse the colloquial sense of 'intention', which means purpose, with the philosophical sense initiated by Brentano.[9] It is the latter usage consistently employed by Kolnai.) Like such predecessors as Meinong and Scheler, he assumes that affective responses are the means by which the human mind apprehends certain qualities in the world, most importantly, those qualities that pertain to the value or disvalue of objects.

Intentionality, for Brentano and his successors, means the 'directedness towards an object' that is characteristic of our mental experience. This simple phrase disguises a multitude of problems, however, in virtue of the fact that we can be directed towards objects even when these objects do not exist (for example when we make errors, or are engaged with the objects described in works of fiction). Moreover, whether we are intentionally directed towards an object is not a simple all-or-nothing affair: thus the detective who is hunting for the murderer may be directed towards one and the same object in a succession of different mental experiences (as *the man I interviewed yesterday, the owner of the dagger found next to the body*, and so on) without being aware of the fact that these objects are one and the same. Brentano was interested especially in the different types of intentional directedness involved in perception, judgment, loving and hating, and so on. He saw the goal of philosophy as providing an exhaustive catalogue of the categories of our mental life. Meinong, we might say, extended Brentano's goal to apply not merely to mental acts as events in people's minds but also to the objects of mental experience. Meinong seeks in his 'theory of objects' to provide a catalogue of all of the various different sorts of objects, both existing and non-existing, actual and possible. The most influential phenomenologist, Edmund Husserl, then seeks to bring together these two complementary concerns of Brentano and

Meinong within a single discipline, a discipline combining both descriptive psychology and descriptive ontology.

It is against this background that we are to understand Kolnai's work. Both Husserl and Kolnai hold that there is a certain intelligible correlation between the structures of mental acts on the one hand and the structures of their objects on the other. Thus we see colors, hear sounds, and so on, and by reflecting upon the structures of our acts directed towards these different sorts of objects we can draw conclusions also about the essential structures manifested by these objects themselves.

The first group of philosophers to embrace Husserl's phenomenological method were gathered together at the very beginning of the twentieth century in Munich. To the first generation of this group belong Max Scheler, Alexander Pfänder, Moritz Geiger, and Adolf Reinach, and to the second generation Dietrich von Hildebrand, the recently canonized Edith Stein, Aurel Kolnai, and the Polish phenomenologist and aesthetician Roman Ingarden. (It was especially in Poland, as a result of Ingarden's influence, that the Munich school continued into the second half of the twentieth century, and one third-generation member of the school is Karol Wojtyła, Pope John Paul II.)

The Munich philosophers believed that Husserl's ideas allowed them to investigate whole new territories of ontological structure hitherto unexplored by philosophy. Husserl himself, as they conceived it, had applied this method in his *Logical Investigations* to the structures of perceptual and judging acts and of the corresponding objects. The Munich phenomenologists now extended this method to other spheres, most impressively in the work of Adolf Reinach who, in his *The A Priori Foundations of Civic Law*, published in the first volume of Husserl's *Jahrbuch* in 1913, described the ontological structures of those varieties of communicative language-use we call *promises*. Reinach thereby anticipated what later came to be known as the theory of speech acts. He details the different ways in which we use language in order to perform different sorts of actions, pointing out how some of these actions have specific legal and ethical consequences in the way in which, for example, a promise gives rise to a mutually correlated claim and obligation.

The importance of the Munich school for the history of the phenomenological movement can be seen in the fact that when, in

1913, Husserl published the first volume of his *Jahrbuch für Philosophie und phänomenologische Forschung* (a journal re-established in America after the war under the title *Philosophy and Phenomenological Research*), his editorial board consisted precisely of the leading figures of the Munich school: Scheler, Pfänder, Geiger, and Reinach. This volume contains, in addition to Reinach's work on promises, a large monograph by Scheler, entitled 'Formalism in Ethics and Material Value Ethics', which is an application of Husserl's phenomenological method to the sphere of value. One after another the members of the Munich school took different areas of human experience and of the associated domain of objects and subjected them to phenomenological investigation. Ingarden, for example, applied the method to our aesthetic experiences and to the associated structures in the realm of works of art.

The most notorious member of the Munich school, and also the most influential, was Max Scheler. It was Scheler, more than anyone else, who was responsible for the adoption by Heidegger of something like the Munich method in his *Being and Time*, a work also first published in Husserl's *Jahrbuch*, where we find phenomenological investigations of the world of objects correlated with our everyday working activity, the world of tools or equipment (of tables, chairs, spoons, forks, shoes, bricks). Scheler developed the idea that feelings serve to provide a cognitive basis for ethics in the same sort of way that thinking provides the cognitive basis for logic. Feelings are a way of coming to know certain entities called values, just as thinking is a way of coming to know certain other entities called facts. (Compare in this connection Pascal's notion of a 'logic of the heart' and, in more recent analytic philosophy, De Sousa's claim that in emotions we perceive axiological properties.[10]) For Scheler emotions are absolutely and unproblematically sensitive to value. Feeling, Scheler held, ought to be accorded equal rights with thinking as a route to or source of knowledge. He thereby extended the phenomenological method from the rather intellectualistic realms in which it had been applied above all by Husserl into the more 'intuitive' territories of feeling and emotion.[11] Thus his phenomenology is a way of doing philosophy which would allow us to grasp the value and significance which in his eyes is endemic to the world of human experience, as contrasted with the Cartesian, 'intellectualist' phenomenology, which one might associate perhaps with Husserl. We

cannot try deliberately to observe these meanings or values in intellectualistic fashion, and we cannot try to use the instruments of logic
and science in order to build up theories about these things. For in
order to use logic or thinking to observe entities of the given sort,
we should have to have grasped them already, and the only way we
can grasp them is via feeling and intuition, or via love and hate.
Kolnai echoes some of this trust in the ability of emotions to reveal
the world in his treatment of disgust.

It is Meinong's terminology, however, that Kolnai draws on at
the very start of his essay when he introduces his subject in terms of
the distinction between *Dasein* and *Sosein*. *Dasein*, a term used also
by Heidegger, means something like 'being there', specifically the
sort of being there, the sort of existence, characteristic of human
beings. It is used by Kolnai to refer to the fact that objects are sometimes immediately present in our surroundings so that they affect
our very being, as in the case of objects of anxiety or fear, also emotions to which Kolnai devotes attention in these essays. Anxiety and
fear, which are both meanings of the German *Angst*, are often taken
to be separate affects, anxiety connoting an amorphous mood more
than an emotion with an intentional object. Kolnai rejects this
approach and treats both together as a single phenomenon. The
interchangeability of terms is confirmed by his later essay, 'The
Standard Modes of Aversion: Fear, Disgust, and Hatred', which he
wrote in English. In 'Der Ekel' the term Kolnai usually chooses is
Angst (anxiety or fear), occasionally *Furcht* (fear). In this translation
the editors have normally rendered the term as 'fear', occasionally
using also 'anxiety' depending on context and ease of idiom, but the
reader should bear in mind that the contrast often carried in English
between the two emotions is not intended. According to Kolnai's
analysis, the states of anxiety and fear are different presentations of
the same emotion; both contrast in the same ways to disgust. He
calls into question the notion of a 'free-floating anxiety' which
would exist in the absence of any intentional object and surmises
that this notion indicates confusion regarding some vague or dis-
persed object rather than no object at all.

Anxiety or fear arises in response to an object that is fearsome.
It is directed not only to that object but also to oneself, since in the
experience of fear, one attends not so much to qualities of the object
as to the very being of that object and the dangers it poses. One

could say that the being of the object and its proximity threaten the being of oneself. The behavior that fear triggers is typically flight, and when fleeing an object one is unlikely to dwell on its particular properties. The intentionality of disgust, in contrast to fear or anxiety, is directed more to the *Sosein*, the 'so-being' of its object, that is, to the qualities of the object as they are presented to our senses—its features, traits, characteristics. The intentional direction of this emotion is almost entirely outward, and its focus on qualities implies a certain aesthetic nature of disgust, as Kolnai observes. By this mention of aesthetic character, Kolnai is not referring to the role disgust can play in artistic experience, though his ideas can well be extended to that field and thereby supplement recent discussions of horror that examine the fascination with blood and putrefaction in art. What Kolnai has in mind, rather, is the Kantian doctrine of the disinterestedness of aesthetic experience, by which is meant that such experience cares little for the actual existence of its object but is wholly occupied with the qualities experienced. Disgust is not one of the more obvious means to apprehend the aesthetic characteristics of objects, and it is a mark of Kolnai's originality that he explored it in these terms. As he points out, the intentional structure of disgust directs our attention so strongly towards the revolting properties of its object as virtually to rivet attention. Disgust is a probing exploration; the tip of its arrow of intentionality "penetrates the object." This character of the intentionality of disgust imparts a complex, Janus-faced feel to the emotion, one that almost savors its object at the same time that it is revolted by it. Thus Kolnai notices the peculiar, perhaps perverse, magnetism of the disgusting from the very start of his analysis.

Kolnai's Approach to Emotions

In the categories of contemporary philosophy, Kolnai's approach allies him with what can be termed broadly the cognitivist camp of emotion theory. Cognitivists hold that emotions facilitate our understanding of the world in a way that coordinates with rational modes of cognition such as judgment and inference.[12] Cognitivism in this sense holds that emotions are not to be understood as mere feelings, agitations, or commotions that occur in the mind, and it is also therefore inappropriate to consider them on the model of sensations such as pleasures or pains. Unlike the latter, emotions 'reach out' towards their objects, and thus they have intentionality. As we have noted, the latter term refers not to purpose or to deliberate intent but rather to the fact that mental phenomena such as emotions and beliefs are 'about' something; they are 'directed towards' some object or other, whether a real object, an imaginary object, or a state of affairs. If I fear spiders, my fear is directed to spiders and they are its intentional object; if I fear ghosts, the intentional object of my fear is ghosts, even in spite of the fact that none exists. If I am worried that the weather will turn bad, the intentional direction of my worry is towards the state of affairs expressed through the proposition that the weather will turn bad. It is important that this specialized sense of 'intention' and 'intentional' be borne in mind to avert misreading Kolnai's text to imply that people might deliberately set out to disgust themselves.

At certain periods in philosophy, emotions have been dismissed as interferences with reason and therefore barriers to knowledge. This was the case during the heyday of the powerful logical positivist tradition that reigned in the first part of the twentieth century, where this view expressed itself also in the so-called emotive theory of ethics, according to which ethical statements have no cognitive content but are merely expressions of the feelings of the speaker. Such opinions have rightly been eclipsed in recent years from philosophical thinking emerging from several directions. These include the revival of Aristotelianism in ethics, attention in epistemology to different means by which ideas may be grasped and formulated, expansion of the scope of philosophy of mind and consciousness, the rise of cognitive science, and even through attention on the part of the philosophically minded to physiological studies of the brain.[13] Certainly Kolnai would agree with what is now the majority view to the effect that emotions are means of obtaining knowledge. Emotions yield a type of cognition that is unavailable by any means other than emotional experience itself. Thus it is not as if emotion would merely supply in a dramatic and affective way information about the world that is also available by other, more rational means. When we are disgusted by an object, we have an immediate apprehension of its qualities and an intuition of its nature to which unaided reason would be blind. This perspective has profound implications for the work in ethical theory which occupied most of Kolnai's philosophical attention, including work which was assembled and edited by some of his London colleagues and published in 1978 in the volume *Ethics, Value, and Reality*.[14] In the latter part of the first of the two essays printed here, the ethical objects of disgust crown his reflections concerning emotional aversions.

There is another, narrower, sense of 'cognitivism' presently in use with which Kolnai sits somewhat less easily. This approach seeks to vindicate the role of emotions in cognition by arguing that emotions are rational insofar as they rest upon warranted beliefs. Anger, for instance is not just a groundless psychic upheaval; it is a response to a belief that one has been wronged. The justifiability of belief and the appropriateness of the emotion in response to that type of belief endow emotions with their cognitive reliability. An approach along these lines is probably the majority view at present within emotion theory—that emotions rest upon a complex set of psychological factors, including relevant beliefs. The latter are assessed for truth and falsity, warrant, justification, and so on, in the same way that any proposition may be. With soundly grounded beliefs one may be assured of having rational and justified emotions that are dependable motives for action. The reliance on beliefs serves several purposes in emotion theory. Perhaps most importantly, it establishes grounds on which emotions can be defended against the extreme claim that they have no epistemic standing and are dangerous and irrational mental episodes that are more likely to distort than to clarify understanding. Certainly some emotional experiences fit this description; the common examples are surges of rage, mawkish sentimentality, and blinding love. These are all deemed unjustified because of an absence of well-founded belief. Without the relevant grounding belief that one has been wronged, for example, the anger one experiences at a supposed wrongdoer is baseless. If one discovers that the belief was in error, the anger ought to disappear (though it may leave behind a residue of agitation). If it does not and rage persists, the subject is truly irrational. Sentimentality is often criticized on the grounds that it indicates a refusal to acknowledge the true nature of its object, endowing it with a value it does not possess.[15] And the distortion of belief that love can cause is commonly acknowledged in the expression 'love is blind'. The requirement that an emotion rest upon a well-founded belief does not insist that the belief be true; that would be too stringent. Grief is an incoherent upheaval without a belief that some terrible event has occurred; but if one has good reason to think that it has, even if one is mistaken, then grief is a completely justified response. Indeed, its absence likely signals that one's understanding of a situation is doubtful. (Recall Aristotle's claim that in order for a person exercising practical reason to attain the virtue of justice, he must feel anger at the proper object and to the proper degree.) The coordination of the intentional objects of beliefs with the intentional objects of emotions yields a way to assess affective responses by means of criteria of reliability and justification. This is one of the shared goals of the several cognitivist perspectives in current emotion theory.[16]

While in certain cases Kolnai would have no argument with this conclusion, his approach is importantly different, for he does not lodge the cognitive component of emotion in any grounding belief. The affective experience itself occasions an understanding of the world, and no analytically separable layer of beliefs is required to give warrant to this particular affective grasp of the situation. Not all emotions, of course, are structurally the same, and few theorists presume that they must be. Indeed, so different are emotions that there is a school of thought that rejects their typology under one genus altogether.[17]

Some philosophers and scientists believe that cognitivism has overreached its grasp and rendered emotions too much like beliefs: too rational, too cognitive—and as a consequence, too human and too far removed from our biological heritage. This approach claims that in their effort to redeem emotions from the charge of epistemic incoherence and moral irrelevance, cognitivists have underestimated the roles of sense experience and desire in emotions and have neglected the degree to which emotional responses are shared with non-human animals.[18] The critics thus emphasize the degree to which at least some emotions are not subject to the override of deliberative faculties and function rather as reactive mechanisms. Philosopher Paul Griffiths divides emotions into three categories: quick-response affect programs, higher-order cognitive emotions, and socially-defined psychological states, concentrating on the first, which are illuminated by scientific studies of the brains and behavior of humans and other animals and by evolutionary theory. Affect programs are biologically based response syndromes that have evolved to cope with the challenges presented by hostile environments.[19] Griffiths's approach minimizes the belief components of the emotions in this category, stressing instead their reactive nature and the fact that they utilize modular, nonrational paths of the brain disjoint from those at work in deliberative reasoning. Disgust is one of the emotions better described as an affect program, along with surprise, anger, fear, sadness, and joy. All of these affects tend to bypass higher, deliberative responses. One may react with fear to objects that one knows are not dangerous, for example non-venomous spiders and snakes, and this reaction may then be nearly impossible to overcome. The triggers of disgust are things that are foul. Its evolutionary benefit is to protect the organism from ingestion of toxic substances and to insert that protection at the earliest possible point, namely when the organism first encounters the object. Griffiths refers to these basic emotions as pancultural. They are subject to a degree of cultural molding, but disgust, fear, and anger are comparatively recalcitrant and difficult to override by deliberation or education. As he puts it, "the affect program states are phylogenetically ancient, informationally encapsulated, reflexlike responses which seem to be insensitive to culture."[20]

Kolnai would disagree with the reductionist tenor of this acount, for he considers disgust an emotion as complex as any other and not to be excluded from the company of higher-order cognitive emotions such as guilt or grief or embarrassment. Kolnai, too, distinguishes among different sorts of emotions, but he does so on more phenomonological grounds. Some are strongly intentional, meaning that their feeling quality reaches powerfully out towards their objects. Some, like vague curiosity or mild irritation, are weakly intentional; they but lightly graze their objects. Disgust is an aversive emotion of the first, forceful sort. Even all aversive emotions are not the same, and one of Kolnai's most careful contributions to emotion theory arises from the meticulous distinctions he draws among fear or anxiety, disgust, and hatred. To assert that basic responses such as disgust are relatively primitive reactions that are immune to the influences of culture and learning is not borne out by reflection on instances of disgust or on the objects that are typically found to be disgusting. Kolnai would approve, however, of Griffiths's account of the immediacy and potency of emotional reactions, for he is attentive to the subjectivity of emotions, including the bodily changes they occasion. He recognizes also with the affect-program theorists a degree of stimulus-response that admits of little control, especially with certain aversions. This feature is especially important in the case of disgust, an emotion marked by unmistakable physical reactions. The involuntary component of disgust leads to consideration of the powerful and central role of the bodily senses in the activation of this emotion.

The Sensuous Nature of Disgust

All theorists of disgust recognize a feature of this emotion that is nearly unique: its requirement that there be a *sensory* experience, of a quite specific type, that triggers the emotion. As William Ian Miller observes, "What the idiom of disgust demands is reference to the senses. It is about what it feels like to touch, see, taste, smell, even on occasion hear, certain things. Disgust cannot dispense with direct reference to the sensory processing of its elicitors. All emotions are launched by some perception; only disgust makes that process of perceiving the core of its enterprise."[21] However, this initial agreement among theorists rapidly gives way to debate over just which sense is the primary conduit for disgust.

Researchers who are chiefly interested in disgust as a mechanism that has evolved for protective response tend to place the sense of taste at the center of the emotion. Darwin, for instance, saw disgust as a response that indicates the opposite of gustatory pleasure, linking it with the rejection of objects that are considered inappropriate to eat.[22] Maximally inappropriate are those objects that are actually toxic to ingest, which is another reason to link the disgust response with taste and with eating. Darwin initiates a line of thinking that considers emotions to be responses that have evolved for certain purposes to ensure the well-being of the species, an approach that fosters a link between the affective reactions of human and non-human animals.[23] Such a perspective tends to minimize the cognitive aspects of emotions and to emphasize their mechanical features, as we have just seen with Griffiths's classification of disgust as an affect program that inhibits ingestion of what is foul. Thus psychologist Paul Rozin, who began his extensive inquiries into disgust with experiments that measured what rats would and would not eat, also considers the core sense of disgust to be taste. (Although Rozin began his research by inferring the qualities of disgust from rats' aversion to foods that made them ill, as it developed he came to interpret human disgust as a recognition of the need to retain barriers between our human and our animal nature. Things that disgust us are things that remind us of our animal origins.)[24] Disgust is thereby seen as a fundamentally *rejecting* emotion. The function of disgust "reduces sensory contact with distasteful substances in the mouth cavity and tends toward expelling those substances."[25] Taste, with its role in eating and drinking, is also the sense closest to the most powerful visceral response to what is disgusting: vomiting.

Other theorists of disgust are more inclined to emphasize smell, and Kolnai belongs to this camp. The objects of taste are more limited than those of smell, he observes, for although the senses of taste and smell are so closely co-ordinated as to function virtually as one sense, we eat relatively little of what enters our olfactory range. Smell occurs with a degree of distance between the experiencing subject and the object of perception, and therefore it has a larger compass than does taste. Yet the objects of smell are within sufficient proximity to threaten and revolt, unlike those of vision or hearing, which may be quite remote. Kolnai sees the intentionality of disgust as reaching out towards objects, and his description of smell vividly pictures a questing nose, searching out its objects, more intimate with them than is the case with objects of vision or hearing, and partaking also in the immediate visceral response of the olfactory sense.

In the realm of touch, too, there are examples of disgusting objects, such as the slithery creatures one steps on while wading in murky ponds. Yet their qualities are not in themselves disgusting, according to Kolnai, who points out that if softness and slipperiness were by nature disgusting then it would be inexplicable that one could ever like aspic. Hearing is virtually free from disgust, although vision, which can take in vivid images of putrefaction and suppuration, provides ample scope for disgusting scenes. Seeing, touching, and smelling all grasp the materiality of objects, which is where the central qualities of the disgusting reside. Disgust is intercategorial, in that its objects may be apprehended by means of different senses, and like the experience of eating it can be directed towards a complex object which spans different sensory modalities. In short, the primary sense of disgust is smell, though other sensory conduits are also commonly involved; in any event, disgust always contains a strong sensory component, real or imaginary, at its core. Proximity is also a feature of the experience of disgust, for by being near a disgusting object one risks contamination. Like infection, disgust spreads—from the disgusting object to the disgusted subject. The recoil induced by this aversion recognizes the danger of being nearby.

The Objects of Disgust

The role of the proximity of the disgusting object engenders speculation about the meaning of the object and why it triggers this particular emotion: whether it threatens, contaminates, scares, or just plain revolts. Among those theorists who have reflected upon the phenomenon of disgust, there is most agreement about the types of objects that trigger this emotion. Kolnai's own list of the disgusting converges with similar rosters advanced by Miller, Sartre, Rozin, Kristeva, and scholars of the horror genre of art. Agreement on objects, however, does not entail agreement about the reasons why these objects provoke disgust.[26] Kolnai analyzes the intentional objects of disgust and those features of objects that typically inspire the peculiar revulsion that is characteristic of this emotion. He itemizes nine exemplary traits of what he terms the "materially disgusting," beginning with putrefaction, excrement, bodily secretions, and dirt, and continuing with disgusting animals, especially insects when they appear with the apparent excess of swarms; foods in certain conditions; human bodies that are too near; exaggerated fertility; disease and deformation. Objects of material disgust share the impression of life gone bad, of flesh turning towards death, and of a primordial and profuse regeneration of life from the muck of decaying organic matter. Things that rot and putrefy become the fuel for maggots and bacteria; insects in swarms give the impression of excessive, mindless generation, of life "senseless, formless, surging." Kolnai refers to this sometimes as a sense of redundancy of life, provoked by the experience of reproduction in excess that lacks the structure of life but merely enacts fecundity—overflow, extravagant profusion far beyond necessity.

In the two decades after Kolnai's article appeared, there were several explorations of disgust by European philosophers that at least in the short run achieved more recognition than his own essay. Kolnai's descriptions anticipated and perhaps even influenced Georges Bataille and the development of his theory of the *informe*, his analysis of social abjection, and his scatological and pornographic writing.[27] (Bataille was familiar with Kolnai's work and kept notes on this essay.)[28] But probably the philosophy that most obviously resonates with Kolnai is Jean-Paul Sartre's existentialism, which hinges on a sense of the disgust and dread that existence itself occasions. Kolnai's reference to revulsion at the very existence of brute life without governing reason sounds similar to the dreadful awareness of facticity expressed in Sartre's writings. Sartre concludes *L'Être et le néant* with a long excursus into the disgusting; his character Roquentin in *La Nausée* is filled with loathing as he realizes the recalcitrant, mindless materiality of things, which merely are, without reason or purpose. So unrestricted is existence by the order of any real categories that the objects of his perception do not even retain their identities but ooze and shift with unsettling indeterminacy. Roquentin's famous encounter with the roots of a chestnut tree indicates how disgust marks an existential epiphany of sorts: "Had I dreamed of this enormous presence? It was there, in the garden, toppled down into the trees, all soft, sticky, soiling everything, all thick, a jelly . . . I hated this ignoble mess. Mounting up, mounting up as high as the sky, spilling over, filling everything with its gelatinous slither . . . I knew it was the World, the naked World suddenly revealing itself, and I choked with rage at this gross, absurd being."[29] Even in this brief quotation one can see that Sartre is treating disgust in terms of a larger phenomenon of revulsion at what he considers the meaninglessness of life, and by comparison Kolnai's cooler treatment, which assiduously distinguishes among types of aversion, is far less inclined to draw the kinds of conclusions that Roquentin finds revealed by his own emotion. Kolnai takes disgust seriously, for it is an emotion that discloses important values; but his approach is more distant and even perhaps more scientific in its tone, reflecting also a sharp contrast in personality and politics between Kolnai and Sartre.

With reference to a more recent generation of thinkers, we can see that Kolnai adumbrates treatments of disgust such as that found in Kristeva's notion of the abject and Miller's summary of the disgusting as 'life soup', a term he coins in *The Anatomy of Disgust*:

What disgusts, startlingly, is the capacity for life, and not just because life implies its correlative death and decay: for it is decay that seems to engender life. Images of decay imperceptibly slide into images of fertility and out again. Death thus horrifies and disgusts not just because it smells revoltingly bad, but because it is not an end to the process of living but part of a cycle of eternal recurrence. The having lived and the living unite to make up the organic world of generative rot—rank, smelling, and upsetting to the touch. The gooey mud, the scummy pond are life soup, fecundity itself: slimy, slippery, wiggling, teeming animal life generating spontaneously from putrefying vegetation.[30]

Kolnai notes the degree to which proximity figures in disgust, for that which disgusts presses too close and therefore might contaminate or infect, threatening the integrity and cleanliness of one's body. Not only decaying or oozing substances but the unwashed bodies of others, as well as those who make unwanted sexual advances, are quite likely to arouse disgust. Kolnai notes the borderline that disgust walks between life and death; disgust records the transition states where the integrity of an organism begins to fall apart, as when a putrefying corpse manifests the change from that which was living and human to a mass of undifferentiated, stinking ooze. The disgusting is, as he puts it, "pregnant with death." In spite of its power to revolt, however, Kolnai does not fold disgust into the recoil of fear. He does not see the apprehension of a threat to one's own self as describing the heart of the emotion of disgust, and in this he differs from those theorists who speculate that the core of this aversion is a recognition that one's self-integrity is in danger of disintegration from the polluting force of the disgusting. Kolnai's notion of disgust is therefore different from Kristeva's notion of the abject, for example. Abjection is a complex emotional response that includes, in addition to disgust, vestiges of fear and desire and a dreadful shadow of the fragility of one's personal identity. Certainly in experiencing disgust we perceive also the threat of the disgusting; but this threat does not present itself with the kind of power that would trigger fear. The object of disgust lingers in consciousness as something disturbing, yet "less than I." In both 'Disgust' and 'The Standard Modes of Aversion' Kolnai assiduously distinguishes disgust from fear and loathing, even while recognizing that in actual experience these emotions often come in bundles. Fear and disgust are twin emotions that together comprise horror and are deliberately exploited in what Carroll calls the "art horror" of movies and stories, as with the gross special effects of horror movies.[31] But the double intentional direction of fear or anxiety—towards both the external object and one's self—is muted in disgust, which is almost wholly directed outwards towards the features of the object. Structurally, these two emotions need to be distinguished, even though they appear so frequently as fused or blended together in actual experience. As Kolnai puts it in the beginning of his essay, fear is focused on the *Dasein* of the object, whereas disgust, the more aesthetic of the two emotions because of its invitation to dwell on the presentational qualities of its object, is directed towards the latter's *Sosein*—to particular features—rather than on the fact of its being. Even though fear and disgust occur together so frequently that they sometimes appear to be a unified experience, Kolnai's meticulous separation of the two that he derives from the application of his phenomenological approach is borne out by certain physiological studies of these emotions: psychologists note that a subject experiencing fear, for instance, has an elevated pulse, while with disgust the heart rate slows.[32] Neurological investigation indicates that recognition of the two emotions is processed at different areas of the brain: the amygdala for fear, the insula and basal ganglia for disgust.[33]

Kolnai's careful study of the fear, disgust, and hatred that is initiated in 'Disgust' and developed more fully in 'The Standard Modes of Aversion' suggests a solution to a troubling observation often made regarding emotions in general, namely, that there seem to be so many more 'negative' than 'positive' emotions (or at least more names for the former than the latter). As negative counterparts of love, for instance, we can name hate, loathing, contempt, abhorrence, abomination. As counterparts of placidity or acceptance there are all manner of varieties of anger: fury, rage, indignation, resentment, exasperation, annoyance, aggravation, and so forth. (The list of anger-related terms is particularly long.) Reflection on the disparity between the relatively short list of positive or happy emotion terms and the huge varieties of negative or aversive emotions, might lead one to uncomfortable conclusions about human nature. But Kolnai supplies us with a matter-of-fact observation about the *objects* of different emotions that circumvents the need for deeper explanations: positive or 'pro' attitudes simply have a wider range of objects than do negative or 'con' attitudes. The latter are more specific, more tied to particular objects. Thus there are no real opposites for emotions (love, hate, and so on). The emotions are asymmetrical, and they only appear to line up as opposites one to another.[34]

Fear, disgust, and hatred are aversions that all serve to bring about recoil and avoidance, but they function differently.[35] Fear is structured to induce flight and rests on the perception of a strong causal nexus between the intentional object and a danger to the subject. Fear is thus keenly aware of its object and of its proximity, but it is not intrinsically interested in its qualities. As we have seen, things are quite different in disgust, where sensible features of objects are presented most vividly, inducing elements of fascination. Like fear, disgust induces avoidance; like hatred, it compels interest. Hatred gives rise to a particularly intense interest in its object; its intention is "inquisitive, aggressive, propulsive." It has an especially palpable historical character that accounts for why a subject hates an object, and therefore it typically has a specific, individual reference. One may hate one or two persons, for example, but few of us hate people in general. For this reason, lists of typically disgusting objects are more readily compiled than lists of objects of hate.

One of the central examples on every theorist's list of the kinds of objects that become disgusting include foods, or more precisely, things that ought to be edible but that for one reason or another affront the senses or the sensibilities of the person involved. Exotic or unfamiliar foods may disgust (ingesting a grasshopper or a snake for many North Americans, for example), even though intrinsically these substances do not evince disgusting qualities. Foods prohibited by dietary laws may appear disgusting to those within a given culture, whereas those who regularly eat such things have a hard time understanding such reactions. Eating arouses both the affront to the senses of taste and smell that are powerful in disgust, and also epitomizes that which can contaminate, for taking a disgusting object into one's body is the most intimate sort of contact and therefore one of the most dangerously polluting.

But Kolnai also notes that there is a spectrum of flavors moving from the attractive to the disgusting, so that by moving along this spectrum attraction may tilt over into aversion—or vice versa. He has in mind the example of high or gamy meat, which is deliberately left unprepared until decay sets in, heightening the fleshy taste and achieving a state of *haut goût*, or 'high flavor'. Strong, ripe cheese has the same effect: the production of a sense experience that skirts the edge of the revolting but is thereby rendered—not marginally acceptable—but actually *better* than the substance would be in a less advanced state. "A slight putrefaction still does not suppress the specific smell and taste of the material in question, but indeed accentuates them to an extent which makes them even more characteristic—the phenomenon of *haut goût*."

The example of *haut goût* is raised several times in Kolnai's essay to account for the paradoxical nature of disgust. The revolting object exerts a certain "macabre attraction" over the subject, leading to a peculiar absorption in the object and lending a magnetism to this aversion. This is Kolnai's route to understanding the apparent element of desire that operates in tandem with aversion in the experience of disgust, a subject of extensive speculation on the part of psychoanalysts as well. Freud, for example, considered disgust a reaction formation that inhibited a subject from acting upon repressed sexual desires. But Kolnai rejects what he considers the 'reductionism' of psychoanalysis. As a good phenomenologist, he prefers instead to direct his analysis of emotions to the conscious regions, whose complexity amply repays attention and, if we are sensitive to the nuances of experience, affords all the answers that we need. Nonetheless, Kolnai appreciates the psychoanalytic recognition of what even he calls the "eroticism of disgust," a breed of aversion which is superimposed "upon the shadow of a desire for union with the object"; this magnetism of the disgusting, as we have seen, is one of its hallmarks. Rather than probing the unconscious, however, Kolnai holds that it is the conscious examination of excessive sensory experiences themselves which suggests the conversion of an attraction into an aversion that still retains traces of the attraction. Think how the paradigm of attraction in taste experience—the sweet—can quickly reach surfeit; and how when indulgence persists, that surfeit cloys and revolts. Here even on a simple sensory level we can see the structure of the disgusting in play. Kolnai's observations here thus anticipate Miller's longer discussion of the varieties of surfeit, both gustatory and sexual.[36] Excessive indulgence of the sensory pleasures is one of the most easily understood conversions of attraction into aversion, and it provides another way to understand Freud's observation that disgust and other reaction formations, including shame and indeed the whole of morality itself, form a crucial curb to the expenditure of human energies in the pursuit of sensuous indulgence. As Kolnai somewhat wryly puts it, disgust prevents us from drowning in pleasure.

Disgust and Moral Apprehension

The most vivid exemplars of material disgust—putrefaction, excessive fecundity without structure, and so on—furnish the language we use to describe the response of disgust that we experience when we encounter morally repugnant persons or situations. Kolnai takes this to indicate something even deeper than linguistic practice: that moral disgust is an important part of an ethical sensibility. It helps us to grasp and to feel aversion towards certain character and behavior flaws (slimy characters, creepy gestures) that require serious attention. But Kolnai's extension of material disgust into the regions of moral judgment has some idiosyncratic elements.

As one might expect, sex figures prominently among those categories of behavior that can be perverted into what is disgusting. The extension of that which is sweet into that which satiates in a disgusting fashion reminds Kolnai of incest, in which love and attraction have outgrown their proper boundaries and become excessive, perverted. The gastric paradigm extends to excessive vitality of other sorts, which are again especially manifest in sexual indulgence. But this is no mere somatophobia on Kolnai's part. Excessive spirituality is just as apt to arouse disgust as is excessive sexuality, and Kolnai (for all his commitment to Catholicism) is no more forgiving of an overabundance of piety than of the lapses of a libertine. Both fail to honor moderation; they flow over and beyond their proper proportions and grow unbalanced. The ensuing loss of structure brings about a squishy inertness liable to grow all manner of moral fungus.

A number of questions may be raised about Kolnai's extension of his analysis of visceral, sensory disgust to morally salient responses. One of the features of the emotion of disgust is its immediacy; unlike contempt (to which it stands in marked contrast), it is not founded on any studied judgment about the moral adequacy of its object. Rather, disgust can itself ground the negative judgment. Disgust is more like a sensitivity to corruption, a sensitivity that is palpable in the case of visceral responses to decay and putrefaction, and that Kolnai sees operating in the moral realm as well. Some readers may consider this expansion unwarranted, or perhaps assume that Kolnai intended a merely metaphorical extension of the language of disgust to the domain of moral judgments. This, however, would fail to do justice to Kolnai's perspective. He regards the capacity to feel disgust to be a matter of our human reactiveness not only to decay and foulness in the sensory realm, but also to moral decay and foulness of character. Disgust, he holds, is an indispensable foundation of our ethical sensibility. Granted, it cannot stand alone: that is, it cannot by itself justify moral condemnation; and there are circumstances that positively require that disgust be overcome. But without the responsiveness of disgust, ethical discernment is withered and impoverished. The degree to which he sees in disgust a moral sensitivity to qualities of personal wrongdoing and corrupt character bears witness to Kolnai's moral realism. But even a committed realist may be taken aback at some of the examples of objects of moral disgust that Kolnai advances, such as the case of a soldier questioning the orders of a superior officer. (Both Elisabeth Gombrich and Elizabeth Kolnai, who drafted earlier English versions of 'Der Ekel' in the period after World War II, glossed over this example in their translations. It is hard not to read in this some shared doubt concerning Aurel Kolnai's estimate of the scope of moral disgust.)

Although Kolnai treats disgust as at least a reliable starting point for moral condemnation, other theorists are more cautious. William Ian Miller and Martha Nussbaum both note the dangerous quality of disgust, which not only recoils from but degrades its object, indicating the peculiar power of this emotion. They have in mind the origin of this emotion in responses to material objects and their sensible features; as Miller puts it "Disgust makes beauty and ugliness a matter of morals."[37] Nussbaum is even more wary, arguing that the content of disgust is always of dubious reliability and has no place in social norms, especially those sanctioned and enforced by law.[38] She observes how frequently the attribute of the disgusting has been attached to social minorities or disempowered groups such as Jews, homosexuals, even women. Disgust has thus served as a tool of injustice by discrediting and condemning the distasteful persons and behavior of others, and has rendered that condemnation all the more powerful by its origin in a strong emotive response. Kolnai does not address this problem extensively, though it is doubtful that this is the use (or misuse) of disgust that he has in mind when he treats disgust as a foundation for moral judgment. Sexual behavior, because of its bodily character, seems to straddle both his categories of the materially and the morally disgusting, and since the former is viscerally so immediate it can lend the latter particularly recalcitrant strength. Nussbaum sees disgust as functioning especially vigorously in the oppression of homosexuals; Miller agrees with Freud that sex of any kind is always disgusting and that initial revulsion must be overcome by love. Kolnai was clearly quite conservative, though not notably squeamish, in his views about sex; several times he mentions unwanted sexual advances—especially male homosexual advances— as examples of disgusting proximity.[39]

Above all, an unreliability of character marks the domain of the morally disgusting, indicating a borderland where firm principles are lost to vacillating whim and to an obsequious accommodation to circumstance. The notion of excess—which implies the presence of a trait that is good at the start but grows out of control and loses its proper structure and boundaries—is at the heart of general moral softness, or of that moral spinelessness that admits virtually anything because it lacks any principles or values of its own. Kolnai hates what he calls "excessive sentimentality," and he expresses this distaste with a vigor that is unexpected given what one might take to be the relative harmlessness of sentimental indulgences, for example as displayed in Kolnai's own favorite case: the emotional blandishments of nineteenth-century Russian literature.[40] Kolnai assails sentimentality for its disparity between the value content of its object and the "stupefying exuberance" of the emotive response; he likens it to a kind of moral *haut goût*, a deliberate cultivation of a taste to a point of perversity. Kolnai notes that even in childhood he was inclined to hate "not only wrong but rosy illusions," and surely rosy illusions are a pitfall of sentimentality.[41] What seems a rather idiosyncratic section of Kolnai's essay might be placed in a more comprehensible context if we bear in mind his own political experience in the period between the writing of the two essays printed here. As we saw above, Kolnai experienced the emotive as well as the political excesses of National Socialism at first hand in the years before he began his circuitous route to exile in North America and England. Excessive sentimentality is an emotional distortion of the value of an intentional object and is the soil for profound moral failings that can have the most far-reaching consequences. Indeed, Kolnai's attack on sentimentality and its dangers is reiterated in the later 'Standard Modes of Aversion'.

A misapprehension of the true nature of an object, event, or situation connects with the other categories of moral disgust: lies, falsehood, betrayal—corruption of the truth in all its forms. Kolnai employs some of his most intense and colorful language in the description of a lie as a "wormlike, crookedly hidden aggressiveness," one that presses upon the lied-to with yet another brand of disgusting proximity. The lie is also a sort of excess, another brand of vitality put to perverse ends, "swimming in vital matter which is at odds with itself." Betrayal, corruption—all these are interpreted as varieties of misdirected life, of surplus vitality resulting in the decay of character.

Excess, redundancy, loss of proper structure in life all form a 'metaphysical datum' that lies at the root of the disgusting. This by no means implies that disgust is a route to moral or normative certainty; in his caution here, Kolnai would agree with Nussbaum. There are situations in which it is morally requisite to overcome initial disgust and readjust one's assessment of a situation. At the same time, disgust is attuned to certain values, a way to discover those real properties that the world presents. (Kolnai follows Meinong and Scheler in their recognition of the real properties of value of which only emotions can provide insight.)[42] Of course disgust may be misdirected. It requires reflection and assessment, as do judgments of reason. Just as impressions of the senses may mislead, so emotions are not free from error. Yet this does not obviate the importance of disgust as a gauge and measure of qualities and values in the world.

Disgust

Disgust

AUREL KOLNAI

Introduction

The problem of disgust has to my knowledge been thus far sorely neglected. In comparison to the scientific (psychological and metaphysical) interest that has been applied to hatred and fear [*Angst*],[1] not to mention aversion or displeasure [*Unlust*], disgust—although a common and important element of our emotional life—is a hitherto unexplored sphere. At best it has been occasionally discussed as a 'higher degree of dislike', as 'nausea', or as 'reaction following upon a repression of urges'. But considered for itself the feeling or attitude of disgust possesses a unique and characteristic quality, which is at one and the same time difficult to clarify and not something which can be taken as a primitive phenomenon of the natural world (like, say, attraction and repulsion). Thus a phenomenological investigation seems here to be highly appropriate. The interest of the subject is enhanced in that disgust has both its own specific accent (in comparison for example with fear) and, in spite of this, extends over a remarkably wide range. Both in the physiological and in the moral sphere we can experience, with very slight differences of coloring, the same 'disgust', or, to put it more sharply, almost the same quality of disgustingness can be present to us. (To what extent the physiological can be said somehow to include the moral sphere should become clearer in the course of our investigation.)

Thus our efforts in what follows will not be confined strictly to the phenomenological sphere: we are dealing here also with both psychological issues and with phenomena belonging to the sphere of

descriptive aesthetics, possibly even to metaphysics. Our investigation has, from the methodological standpoint, an exclusively phenomenological aim, that is to say, the aim of seeking to grasp the
essence, the significance and the intention of disgust, and also what
might be called the law of cohesion of its object-realm—to which
our incidental illumination of these other matters can only be con-
ducive. This we attempt primarily in light of a parallel with the
notion of fear. Finally we shall investigate briefly the significance of
disgust in reference to ethics.

I. On the Delimitation of Disgust

I.1. *Points of View*

Disgust belongs to the category of so-called 'defense reactions' or,
to put it more delicately, to the modes of aversion alongside dislike,
hate, sorrow (felt about something), or shuddering (at something),
and many others. Conceptual distinctions can be pursued from a
number of points of view. We shall select here seven such points of
view, without wishing to deny that a closer interrelation exists
among some than among others, nor to imply that they are by any
means the only possible ones.

(a) ACCORDING TO THE RANGE OF ITS OBJECT

Disgust is never related to inorganic or non-biological matter,[2] a
restriction which applies neither to fear nor to dislike. Hatred and
contempt on the other hand have an even narrower object-range.
Moreover, in spite of the more markedly ethical determination of the
objects of contempt, there is nevertheless a class of types of attitude,
towards which contempt—though not hate, in its primary sense—
may be directed. Fatuous thinking may arouse contempt, or a feeling
of being ill at ease, but not disgust; what is known to be not dangerous cannot, in general, give rise to fear, but it may still be disgusting.

(b) ACCORDING TO MODE OF INTENTIONALITY

The moment of intentionality stands in the foreground in hate and
contempt, less so in cases of disgust, less still, perhaps, in cases of

anger, and it declines to a minimum degree in feelings of ill will and of uneasiness.[3] It is the nature of the intending—of what is meant or intended in an experience—that will occupy us in particular. A further type of fluctuation in degree of intentionality is to be found in sorrow and also—though structured in a totally different way—in fear. A genuine absence of intentionality is possible in cases of mere displeasure [*Unlust*].

(c) ACCORDING TO THE CONDITION [*ZUSTÄNDLICHKEIT*] OF THE SUBJECT[4]

This is not merely the complement of the factor of intentionality. Thus hate is certainly more of a state or condition of the subject than is contempt, disgust more than hate, anger more than disgust. Yet anger conditions the subject fully and is not somehow less conditional than feelings of ill will, because it is more a modality of the entire condition of the person.

(d) ACCORDING TO IMMEDIACY OR PRIMORDIALITY

The defense reaction can be determined to a greater or lesser extent by our knowledge and by our established firm attitudes towards values. This can be in inverse proportion to their degree of immediacy or primordiality. 'Contempt' and 'malaise' are here also the two endpoints of the series. Though disgust is more sharply intentional than anger, it is at the same time also more primordial than the latter, because it turns more on impressions than on the grasping of states of affairs. And disgust is, further, more immediate and more sensual than abhorrence, even physical abhorrence, because by its very nature the latter presupposes to a greater extent some kind of conscious justification, depends more on acquired knowledge. (Consider for example our abhorrence of flies as carriers of disease.)

(e) ACCORDING TO DEGREE OF INDEPENDENCE

Not quite equal in meaning with the above is the degree of independence as opposed to dependence on other concomitant defense reactions. Fear is hardly a more immediate reaction than disgust; it is however more independent since every feeling of disgust, without

necessarily including fear, yet alludes to it somehow. Indeed, it is
sometimes—falsely, but not without foundation—taken as a variant
of fear. Contempt, in contrast, at least in most of its forms, incon-
testably involves a reference to disgust. Conversely psychic components of a moral sort can also contribute to an aversion of a more
physical sort, as for example when hate and contempt color a feeling
of abhorrence.

(f) ACCORDING TO DEGREE OF LINKAGE TO THE BODY

In connection with disgust one thinks of the two opposite poles of
contempt and nausea. Hate and even anger are less bound up with
bodily phenomena than is disgust, in spite of the more violent
physical phenomena attendant upon anger. This is because the sensuous impressions involved in disgust and the suggestion of a physical reaction of vomiting play here a more essential role in a way
that is much more specific and concrete than the raging, kicking,
and throwing which may arise through anger. Every kind of disgust—even moral disgust—is, even if not more physical, still somehow more physiological than anger. On the other hand disgust
should not be confounded with nausea as such, nor with the tactile sensations connected with the latter (especially the sticky, the
clammy, or the lukewarm). However there is a sense in which fear
is even more bound to states of the body than disgust: for once any
feeling of fear, in contrast to disgust, has been related to something physical, it thereby becomes also directed to the body itself
and to its 'intactness'.

(g) ACCORDING TO RESPONSE-CHARACTER

Hate, a highly intentional phenomenon, and uneasiness, which is
hardly intentional at all, resemble each other in this respect: that
both have a relatively weak response-character and are more 'spontaneous': the one searching, choosing, pursuing, the other as it were
growing and rising. Fear and disgust are in contrast genuine 'reactions'; they are to some extent and according to their intention
'appropriate' responses to disturbing influences. There are, it is true,
feelings of fear (but not of hate) without conscious cause, but this
does not affect the essential character of *every* case of fear: fear is pre-

cisely fear in face of 'something' which itself compels that fear—a something which then acquires its givenness, its stamp, from this fear, and which is perhaps represented by more harmless objects (phobias). Notwithstanding the higher degree of intentionality of hatred, the quality of frightfulness and disgustingness exist objectively as 'releasers' of determinate types of reactions in a way which cannot be compared with any quality of hatefulness; hate goes directly for what is hostile or evil, for the threat.

I.2 *Disgust and Fear as the Principal Types of Defense Reaction*

Disgust and fear seem, however, to form a pair, whose mutual correlation will allow us, through the elaboration of the differences between them, to learn more about the nature of disgust. This is particularly so because fear presents a comparatively simpler phenomenon. Fear and disgust have this in common, that they are both simultaneously intentional and conditional; they have in common approximately the same degree of immediacy, and also the character of being in a narrower sense attitudes of defense. Nausea, shuddering, though also closely entangled with psychical phenomena, are by no means feelings in the strictest sense. And in contrast with, say, dislike, both fear and disgust manifest a close linkage with the body and—not independently of this—a psychic 'depth', a power which, at least temporarily, fills out the personality. Finally we have suggested that there is a certain relation of contents according to which—in a way not yet fully specified—whatever is disgusting might also cause fear.

Before the parallels with fear are investigated, however we wish to emphasize further the special character of disgust in contrast to certain related modes of reaction.

(a) Disgust is to be contrasted with *contempt*—not only with the contempt that is rooted in the corporeal sphere, but also with contempt in the moral sphere—as will be made clear in Section IV.1.

(b) Disgust is not accentuated *displeasure*. It is certainly true that highly accentuated displeasure tends, like disgust, to call forth the tonalities of the repulsive, or precisely: the disgusting. It is no accident that vulgar exaggeration light-heartedly refers to hateful and unpleasant things as 'disgusting', just as it calls things which are

unattractive, disagreeable or burdensome—and even what is simply
powerful, large or important—'frightful' and 'horrible'. (Compare
Section II.) But displeasure has in itself nothing to do with disgust;
for there is a certain kind of extreme displeasure which contains little or nothing of disgust (the 'repulsive') and yet on the other hand
there is a kind of weak feeling of disgust, which is still real disgust
(the weak, sweet smell of decay). We may even experience disgust
towards objects that we do not find simply aesthetically repellent
(for example certain insects). Disgust is in general more attached to
the body, perhaps also more ethically related, than is displeasure; but
it is neither such a general nor such an aesthetically oriented category as displeasure. It is in fact a *defense reaction* in a quite different
and narrower sense. But it should already be admitted here that disgust is more aesthetically determined than is fear. (Aesthetics relates
to the features, to the so-being [*Sosein*] of the object; see Section
II.3.)

(c) *Abhorrence* is a derivative of a higher order, something that
presupposes and is built upon disgust, fear, and concrete value-ori-
ented attitudes [*Werthaltungen*].

(d) It is more difficult to differentiate from disgust the tonalities
of the repulsive, or even of the disagreeable or *loathsome*. Frequently
the latter connotes an incomplete and somehow more formal disgust. One can only be repelled—in the strict sense—by things that
do not have the characteristic of the disgusting: for instance, food
which is neither spoiled nor personally detested, but which rather for
some unknown reason just fails to be tasty. In such cases what one
might call the objective contours of disgust are missing. An object
may be repugnant to me on account of some mere fleeting association, but yet I do not therefore find it 'disgusting'. (See Section III.
on the notion of satiety.)

(e) It would be completely mistaken to interpret disgust as an
attenuated nausea. There can be no talk of such a simple bodily
functionality in the case of disgust. Thus in spite of the clear allusion
to nausea which is inherent in all disgust, there exist very strong feelings of disgust with only a trace of actual nausea, namely in those
cases where disgust is not mediated by impressions of taste or smell.
And there is on the other hand strong nausea without any overwhelming degree of disgust. Even in some cases there is nausea
without any but the slightest degree of proper disgust at all, whether

these be cases of illness—somatic 'nausea' can be entirely free of disgust—or certain cases of extraneous mechanical influence. Nausea may result from corrosive gases or from insertion into the mouth of certain unpalatable (inorganic) objects that induce violent vomiting movements without inducing feelings of disgust. Thus although disgust presupposes nausea (compare fear and flight, Section II), it is itself neither a type of nausea, nor a suppressed form. The supposition that disgust is merely a mixture of nausea and contempt is nothing but a cheap, unphenomenological jest. There is also disgust that on the physical side is tuned more towards the shudder than any actual vomiting (disgust which is closest kin to fear, usually aroused by visual impressions).

We might well be asked why we have not, in our effort to distinguish disgust and fear, taken into consideration any parallel differences between the positive, pleasurable emotions that correspond to them. Our answer will be that such exactly corresponding responses do not exist. Desire, pleasure, affirmation, sympathy do indeed mirror aversion, displeasure, negation, and antipathy as symmetrical contrasts, but such comparisons are shifting and lose their validity as soon as we leave the sphere of formal, direction-designating structures. Love and hate themselves are by no means such congruent contrasting images of each other. The contrary opposite of love is disgust no less than hate, and ethical love of what is good does not correspond simply to hate of what is evil. And if we try to conceive, say, trust, reliance, or confidence as opposites of fear, then the very attempt shows already the weakness of the presupposition of a symmetrical relation between opposites. Neither desire, nor liking, nor attraction is an adequate opposite of disgust. The tonality 'appetizing', on the other hand, although of more substantial content, would be too narrow for what we need here. Thus it seems to be the case, that, while the unpleasurable reactions differentiate themselves quite sharply into distinct types (hate, fear, disgust), there is on the positive side the more unified attitude of love, which then becomes transformed in various ways not completely parallel to the negative forms. On the metaphysical origin of this difference we may perhaps conjecture that the act of affirmation is a more unbroken, direct expression of the total life of the subject which is only secondarily colored by the various functions and objects towards which it is adapted (love is more colored by the object than is hate).

Whereas the act of negation—already 'dialectical' in its nascent state—has to 'justify' itself, even in its most general form, by expressing especially the kind of damage which the subject has suffered.

II. Fear and Disgust

II.1. *The Intentional Content of Fear and Anxiety*

The term 'anxiety' [*Angst*] is used here not in such a way as to suggest any strict distinction between anxiety and fear [*Furcht*], so that we do not wish to exclude from our observations for example cases of fear brought about by objects that really are dangerous. Certainly one can understand by anxiety in a narrower sense a kind of unmotivated, more or less 'free-floating' state of fear, not strictly related to any object; we however shall use the word in a wider sense, preferring it to the term 'fear' only in order to keep in play the image of the full, 'redundant' feeling of fear (*'pavor'*), in contrast to the concept of fear as a mere 'worrying' about an unwelcome event or as a presumption of a danger (*'timor'*). In general we have in mind only the 'normal', object-directed anxiety as such, anxiety *in face of something* (even if it is not in every case proportional to that thing).

The mode of intending characteristic of fear or anxiety is twofold. It intends at one and the same time two completely separate objects: what provokes it and the subject who experiences it.[5] I experience anxiety or fear when something threatening appears or when I think about it; but this clearly only in regard to myself, my own person. Whether it is in a given case a matter of my existence, of my interest, of my eternal salvation, or of other, alien interests which are yet dear to me, is here completely irrelevant to the peculiar directedness of the intention in question. It may not however be irrelevant insofar as the most typical state of fear is founded in the self; fear for another's, a beloved person's sake is already something which involves a more complicated kind of emotion.

There is a view that genuine, instinctive fear does not rest on such a concern for one's self but is merely an immediate 'taking fright' before what has provoked it, and that fear is in no way any kind of 'short cut' to the threat of one's own welfare. We hold this view to be merely an expression of that fashionable type of irrationalism which, shy of the notion of 'causal determination' and of any 'utilitarian shallowness', will hear nothing of a connection between sexual lust and procreation or between hunger and food. Certainly, fear is not to be compared to, say, a cautious merchant's unfavorable appraisal of his own chances of profit, but what is *meant* in it is in every case the subject's own good or ill. Every kind of *flight* from something has a strictly teleological intent, but flight is merely the instinctive culmination, the discharge of fear. The concept of fear is inseparable from that of threat, danger, rescue and need of protection. Empirically this is not something that stands in need of verification. Proof—if proof were needed—is provided by the fact that, as soon as we know ourselves to be in complete security from something threatening, fear decreases to the level of a slight shivering [*gruseln*]. This is hardly even 'weak fear' any more. The ease with which the instinct of fear can be rationally controlled through knowledge of the factual situation is demonstrated by our behavior in front of cages containing dangerous animals: nearly all trace of fear is absent. The fear which remains after enemies have been subdued, which significantly enough often approximates to an unclear type of oppression, is after all, rarely accompanied by a true conviction that in this matter all danger is really over.

The double intention previously mentioned exists also in certain marginal cases that are less clear, for instance when I am afraid of myself. Nothing is more obvious than the intentional division of the self in this case—and this does not mean a division into an ideal or formal self and a material or essential self of the type which may occur in self-contempt, but rather a division of the material, acting ego itself, whereby the 'superior' willing part, anchored in an interest in one's own welfare or morality, is threatened by more primitive passions. And no less subjected to this double intention is 'object-less' or 'free-floating' fear or anxiety, where the reflexive relation towards one's own self is of a greater psychic strength and plays a more dominant conscious role. For what is alien and threatening can be so much more profoundly experienced when it is unknown and unidentifiable, when its nature can be only conjectured. Free-floating fear or anxiety of this kind is radically different from any mere weariness of life or general malaise. One need only think of one's fear of the dark, which has such a vivid character of being fear of something, which is yet clearly neither a simple fear *of* the dark, nor

Aurel Kolnai

a fear of, say, robbers or ghosts. And it is indeed, undoubtedly true that even something undefinable—though certainly only in the rarest of cases completely undefined!—may be intended.

But what is it that holds this double intention together? Is it that the threatening object and one's self are experienced as a single entity, as sometimes happens in a certain sense in cases of feelings of community? Certainly not; the real linkage between the two poles of intention can also be a purely accidental one. The intention is much more directed towards the relevant factual relation [*Sachverhalts-beziehung*], and towards this merely as something 'pure' and actual, not as something which might constistute an essence, as for example historical relations do. For the intention of fear is characterized by a certain abstractness and an indifference to the intrinsic nature of things: what is dangerous is there before us only as 'danger', and one's own self is intended principally as a unity of existence only. Thus in contrast to hate, fear does not 'pursue' its object through to its individual facets; it does not evaluate it, nor permeate its nature with a web of intentions. And in contrast to the uneasy anxiety about something, fear never singles out, in the first place, particular spheres of interest in one's own self: for in every genuine case of fear it is somehow the whole self, or the very existence of the self, which is put in question, whether it is one's very life which is threatened, or whether it is the salvation of one's soul, one's livelihood, social position or personal liberty or even one's innocence that as it were fills out or represents the content of this existence. Even if fear be particularly weak because of the distance or uncertain effectiveness of what provokes it, still its intentional directedness always somehow 'permeates through' to the most ultimate and vital interests which appear to be endangered. But however much fear may seem to direct itself back in this way towards the subject, this does not mean that it lacks a certain intuitive grasp of its object. States of affairs are after all not in themselves fear-provoking—as they can be, say, unpleasant, mysterious, or unbearable. It is objects, images, circumstances, events existing with the subject in their relation to each other in a state of affairs that provoke fear. A tiger remains a 'fearsome' animal even behind iron bars, and if in spite of this the sight of him does not evoke any actual fear, then this is an immediate consequence of a fear-inhibiting consciousness of the state of affairs that 'there is an obstruction which protects me from him'. The decisive effect of the experience of such states of affairs is not of course a characteristic of all feelings, but belongs particularly to the case of fear.

II.2. *The Intentional Content of Disgust*

Disgust distinguishes itself from fear fundamentally with regard to the direction of intention. The intention of disgust is much more markedly orientated outwards: in spite of its strong physiological effect, disgust lacks the powerful, inwardly-aimed intentional flowing backwards of the sort which we find in cases of fear. And disgust is distinguished also, though quite differently, by the way in which it adheres to the object which is its cause; this object is grasped in an incomparably less schematic and also less dynamical manner that is more saturated and concerned more with the minutiae of the object. It is not—as in the case of fear—the relation to a state of affairs involving the subject's survival which is constitutive of the object or of its mode of givenness, but rather this object's own intrinsic constitution. In order to comprehend fully the difference, consider how, in the typical course of development, states of fear and of disgust are terminated. In the former case when the threatening object has been 'sighted' it continues to be intentionally the same while the developing feeling relates more intensely to the subject's own self and his condition and future fate: thus the threatening object forms the constant backdrop to the moving play of intentions about the person's self. The reverse is true in the case of disgust: from the very beginning there is shuddering and a turning away from the object, and nausea, either real or intentional. These phenomena may increase in intensity with the continued presence of the disgusting object, and they may get 'darker' in tone, but the tip of the intention penetrates the object, probing and analyzing it, as it were, and becoming immersed in its motions or in its persistence, in spite of essential hesitations and a reluctance which may, of course, also lead to a sudden cessation of contact with the object and thereby a disappearance of disgust. Thus disgust may have a cognitive role that is lacking in cases of fear; fear may lead to the apprehension of a danger, but disgust has the power to impart directly what may be very clear-sighted partial awareness of its object, which may be quite intuitive in nature.

At the same time the intending which is involved in disgust is more uniform. Here there are not two poles, an image-like object-pole and an experience-reabsorbing pole, bound together in a determinate factual relation. Rather, an object is intended in 'pictorial' fullness and through the fact that it is intended at all on the given occasion [*Anlass*] it comes to belong to the 'surroundings' of the subject—who is himself then presupposed as a sort of background. The occasion, now, is nothing other than the *proximity* of the object in question, a concept that acquires a central position for the problem of disgust. For proximity is of course not merely an occasion; it is itself also a concurrent object of the disgust sensation. As factual relation it forms a bridge between the provoking object and the subject of a feeling of disgust. But as such it serves a factual relation in a far less pronounced way than in the case of that dynamic causal relation between provocation and subject that is characteristic of fear. The graphic character of the object, the unity of the qualitative features [*Soseins-Einheitlichkeit*] of the whole phenomenon are thus preserved in a far more intact form than in cases of fear. There is a visible character of 'disgustingness' which exists in an entirely different and fuller sense than in any visible character of 'fearsomeness'. How much the moment of proximity enters into this character is shown by the observation that even what are objectively uncaused, fantasy-like feelings of disgust—whether these are provoked voluntarily or are matters of obsession—tend as far as possible to place the object of disgust emphatically in immediate proximity to the subject, in the most immediate sphere of experience of his or her sense organs. All in all, what concerns the state of affairs is here more closely bonded to the image-content of the intention. The matter is not, however, a simple one, and further research will reveal certain further complexities.

The greater unity of the intention proves also to be conditioned by the fact that, in contrast to fear, the feeling of disgust is a peripheral feeling, in that it reaches out to the subject peripherally, as it were, along the surface of his skin, up to his sensory organs and, in a different form, as a kind of secondary intention, to his upper digestive tract and even, with some reservations, to his heart. Even so, it does not reach the subject as a whole, does not pervade the totality of his existence. The location of the subject and the disgust-arousing object merge together, as it were, to constitute what might, somewhat crudely, be called a harmonious unity. This unity will involve also the material side of disgust. For it is not merely the case that the proximity of what is disgusting determines its effect in a high degree; it is rather that one particular aspect of proximity con- stitutes—though by no means alone—the character of disgust. This is its will to be near, its non-self-containedness, or, as I would rather put it, its shameless and unrestrained forcing itself upon us. The dis- gusting object grins and smirks and stinks menacingly at us. The way in which it achieves these effects and their associated responses will throw further light upon the moment of proximity.

The way in which the disgusting object makes itself felt is dif- ferent from the mode of imposition of a hateful object. As has been already mentioned, the latter does not exist as an independent com- mon quality, for hate can be evoked by something which calls forth ethical disapproval, by hostile behavior, by rejection of an amorous approach, and so forth. And instead of hate under similar external circumstances it might be contempt, the desire to improve, fear, grief, which establishes itself as the central emotion. Thus while hate involves a completely spontaneous picking out or choosing of the object, disgust normally arises completely unequivocally as the only possible direct reaction to the object in question. Here it is the object's behavior that is provocative: it forces itself upon us with greater intensity than an object of hatred (and this is true even though hate directed towards wholly distant objects is rare). Indeed it almost seems as if the object of disgust would itself somehow reach out to the affected subject. There is however no hint of per- secution or threat as there is in the case of objects which give rise to fear. This is the paradox of disgust: like anxiety or fear it is a genuine passive defense reaction of the subject in regard to an affect which is unambiguously directed towards him or her. It reaches out, as it were, to the subject. Yet, like hate, once provoked it searches out the object in its whole essentiality instead of developing according to the subject's own personal condition. Where fear aims to become free of, to separate itself from the object, and hate tries either to annihi- late, or at least to weaken or transform its object, disgust holds something of a middle position. Certainly in respect to its *manifes- tations*, the *action* to which it gives rise involves more the intention of removing the object of disgust out of the environment of the sub- ject in order to leave the latter 'in peace'; but in regard to manner of execution, the preparatory active intention in disgust is of an essentially different nature from that of cases of fear. For whereas fear intends its object as something threatening, as something 'stronger than myself' (even in those cases where I feel that I can, if necessary, repel the attack, even overpower the attacker), there is in an intention of disgust a certain low evaluation of its object, a feeling of superiority. What is disgusting is in principle not threatening, but rather *disturbing*, even though a mere disturbance by itself, however strong, cannot evoke disgust. A thing which is perceived as disgusting will always be something which is not going to be regarded as important, which is neither to be destroyed, nor something from which one has to flee, but which must rather be put out of the way. That is to say, where fear coerces me principally to retreat from my surroundings, to alter my circumstances or my situation, disgust leads me much more to a cleaning up of my surroundings, to a weeding out of what is disgusting therein. Still this too determines a turning-outwards and a certain 'seizing' of the object.

Something else arises here which may serve further to illuminate the paradox of disgust. The *challenge* inherent in cases of disgust has an entirely different meaning from that of a threat, even a feeble, ridiculous threat, or of a simple disturbance (either of one's work or of the ordering of one's life). There is without doubt a certain invitation hidden in disgust as a partial element, I might say, a certain macabre allure. This may sound unphenomenological and unmistakably psychoanalytical; and indeed I am here following a psychoanalytical train of thought. But I hope nevertheless to keep phenomenological ground beneath my feet. For there is nothing to which I feel more immune than the dark spells of paradox-ridden psychologistic reductions seeking to 'interpret' each and every case of hate as 'repressed' love, each and every case of love as 'overcompensated' hate. However there *does* exist something like love which becomes reinforced through the suppression of an impulse of hate directed to the same object, although here a peculiar accent will be present, be this a certain constraint or a refined and austere pathos. Now, as will become clear in the treatment of the more substantial aspects of our theme, not only is an aversion to its object characteristic of disgust, but also a superimposed attractedness of the subject towards that object. It should however be noted that—as psychoanalysis may have already ascertained—the intention to vomit which is involved in disgust seems to verify this claim directly. For just as the desire to take flight obviously presupposes that the threatening object may come into my vicinity, or at least affect me in some way, so also the desire to vomit presupposes that the abhorred object might somehow enter my mouth or stomach. And likewise any shuddering of disgust is manifestly less bodily or physiologically determined than in cases of anxiety or fear and therefore more intentional (mental). It also presupposes a possible contact with the disgusting object, a contact which could perhaps be brought about only by myself and not at all by that object. Fear too may exist as it were side by side with a covert 'repressed' desire for the object, but it seems to us that the theories of psychoanalysis concerning this are vastly exaggerated and remote from the essence of the matter. We would be able to find an admixture of yearning in the purest cases of fear only if there existed a general background of desire for self-sacrifice, self-dissolution or self-annihilation, that is to say only by adopting a questionable and far-fetched metaphysical supposition which is for the most part irrelevant to the thing itself. Or does one wish to assert that the paralyzing effect of fear reveals a will to self-surrender, a will to suffer the danger? Does it not rest simply upon an automatic, partial anticipation of the danger, free from any kind of attraction or desire [*Lust*]? However many moments of desire may adhere as secondary elements in cases of fear and danger, fear is in its essence fully understandable without any assumption of a mystical wish for the possession of what is feared.

The case of disgust is however totally different: there is contained already in its inner logic a possibility of a positive laying hold of the object, whether by touching, consuming or embracing it. Already at this point we shall need to underline the relative narrowness of the range of objects of disgust: it contains to a large extent only those entities which would otherwise be destined for a positive use or a determinate kind of contact (foods, living beings). In psychoanalytical terms, disgust is more immediately *ambivalent* than fear. It presupposes, as it were by definition, an (albeit suppressed) desire [*Lust*] for the object which provokes it. This is not at all to imply that disgust is nothing but an expression or a consequence of this suppression, or that it is nothing but the desire itself. The ambivalence is characteristic of only one side of disgust; we shall soon consider other circumstances that will reveal to us the nature of disgust in quite different colors. At all events our having uncovered this moment of ambivalence—which is also present in the phenomenon of satiety (compare the way in which a *sweet taste* may become disgusting, in Section III)—will contribute to our understanding of the curious enticement which forms the starting point of disgust and thereby help to explain the peculiarity of the intention of disgust, that although disgust is triggered as a defense against the object, its subject yet finds himself turning towards the reality which is that object, not towards the existential complex which is his own deliverance.

II.3. *The Relations of Being and So-Being Involved in Fear and Disgust*

It emerges from the foregoing investigations that the intention of fear is, roughly speaking, principally directed towards *being*, towards the existential situation [*Daseinslage*] which confronts us and the intention of disgust principally towards features of the object, towards a type of *so-being* [*Soseinsart*]. We should however add immediately that in fear too this existential situation itself congeals to some extent in the so-being of the feared object, while in the case of disgust the type of so-being is fixed through the existential factor of proximity, through the pertinent environment of the subject.

Several things speak in favor of a primary intention towards existence [*Daseinsintention*] on the part of fear and of a primary intention towards so-being, towards the specific features of the presented object, on the part of disgust. Fear is incomparably more pervasive of the subject, encroaching much further upon his or her total emotional condition, than is disgust. The relation to a state of affairs involves in the one case a genuine relation to existence, where in the other case it is merely a matter of a relation to, as it were, an accidental cross-section of existence. Both fear and disgust have external objects as their focal point, but only disgust rests with, remains focused on, the external objects and on their nature: fear moves on to intend rather an existential change in the subject person under their causal influence. Fear resembles hate in being bound up with the claim to existence, with a will towards certain states of affairs of its intention; disgust resembles hate in regard to their common penetration of the alien object. Fear ranks on the one hand with being afraid and with non-willing and on the other hand with wanting something and with the urge to self-affirmation; disgust, however, is ranked with dislike. In the case of fear, the sensation is primarily a matter of information, for disgust it is primarily an immediate object; only secondarily does there exist on the one side a unified (perhaps visible) quality of being 'fearsome' and on the other side a bringing about or intensification of disgust through association. As opposite of fear we may count the wish; as opposite of disgust, appetite or, better, appetite for a particular thing, a 'craving'. Immediately however we feel that these 'opposites' are relations of different structure: as hate of something would correspond to love for something which was, as it were, objectively opposite, so fear before something would correspond to a wish for something which was subjectively opposite (that is, something helpful instead of something threatening). But in regard to disgust at something, that for which we have an appetite may be somehow similar to the object of disgust which indeed need not in itself be disgusting at all (compare ambivalence). In the whole intentional nexus of disgust we notice, at least from the formal point of view, the exclusion of a dynamic existential element. And this corresponds to the role of the rejecting judgement of *taste* in the arousal of disgust.

Because fear and disgust are both defense reactions, they intend essentially neither alien beings (as do hate, aggression), nor the subject's own so-being (as in contrition, shame). Both are directed rather toward a disturbance of the existence of the subject brought about by alien existing objects. They differ in that for fear the existential circumstances and tendencies of the extraneous being are what is primary and constitutive of its so-being, whereas for disgust the object's entire stock of features [*Soseinsgehalt*] is the primary determining factor, which is connected to no more than a thin thread of actual existence—but which has also a wider, more nebulous existential background, which only investigations into the content of disgust will be able to clarify. Intention towards alien existence can follow only in a purely derivative way in the defense reaction founded in disgust and fear, while the intention of hate moves with a single leap from the so-being to the being of its object; indeed in this sense it does not separate being and so-being at all. For this reason also there is no distinguished quality of something being hateworthy, and therefore also a fantasized hate is much less possible than are fantasized feelings of fear or disgust. (Hate, more than fear or disgust, posits its object as 'real', takes it incomparably more seriously.) And phenomena such as fear or disgust can likewise be directed only secondarily towards oneself, towards one's own make-up. For incomparably more than in the case of, say, contrition and shame, this is a matter of something 'alien in oneself'—leaving quite out of account cases of disgust at, say, one's own bodily infirmity. The quality of contrition and shame could not be derived at all from the disapproval of some alien action with an additional intention towards oneself.

The remarkably close relationship of disgust to positive contact and to the possibility of an affirmative grasping of the object (its ambivalence), the relatively delayed point of bifurcation of acceptance and rejection are all related to the fact that the core of disgust is formally an experience of so-being, involving what is after all an initial attraction to the object. Whereas fear issues from a concern about the subject's existence, the questionable alien object announces itself directly already in its nascent state as something threatening and to be avoided. (In hate, again, the 'initial affirmation' is absent; here there is no direct reaction of feelings, and the functional turning of the attention towards the object is not represented in the emotionally charged image of the object itself, as it is in disgust. Hatred contains the pronounced intentional moments of seeking out, attacking and annihilating, but disgust contains only a moment of turning of the attention towards the object, which is as it were superimposed upon the shadow of a desire for union with the object.) In the case of disgust, too, there lies at bottom a general intention towards existence; only on the strength of such an intention can disgust come about at all, because disturbance presupposes the intention of one's own existence. (Only this intention is not primary nor, in a formative sense, decisive as it is in cases of fear.) For this reason disgust has often been apprehended as a mere variant of fear—a conception whereby we should somehow also experience fear of what is disgusting, a fear which is however characterized by a peculiar additional quality. Many disgusting objects are, as is well-known, harmful or dangerous, yet without displaying directly that open gesture of threat which belongs to what is fearful in the narrowest sense, such as those forces of nature, living beings, and events by which human beings can be seized and crushed. It is much more things such as spoiled food or certain noxious insects that would be disgusting. But this conception is not tenable, for there is a well-known mode of fear or anxiety that pertains to concealed and nebulous dangers without having anything to do with disgust at all. In order to produce disgust, elements are required which are totally different from those which produce insidious threats, and the latter may be entirely absent in the presence of disgusting objects. We may nevertheless maintain this much, that the object of disgust is prone to be connected with something which is concealed, secretive, multilayered, uncanny, sinister, as well as with something which is shameless, obtrusive, and alluring; that is, in sum, to be something which is taunting. Everything that is disgusting has in it something which is at one and the same time both striking and veiled, as is, say, a poisonous red berry or a garishly made-up face. We will perhaps be able to do somewhat more justice to this moment of disgust in our elaboration of its substantial content. What matters here is only to indicate that in disgust, too, there is a quite specific, perhaps not only wholly general, existential intention (intention towards *Dasein*) which constitutes the frame of its tonality as defense. This involves a moment of 'disturbance', a moment of being something which as it were 'flows' from the object's so-being and of obtrusive proximity, yet it involves also a certain reserve, a certain lurking on the side of the object, and thus here too, the tonality of defense is not absolutely lacking in a certain back-reference towards the subject's own existence and safety.

The moment of so-being, on the other hand, does assert its rights in the case of fear in that the image of the feared object there does play the role of a fixed fulcrum of intentionality, even though also the feeling of fear encompasses from the beginning an intention towards the condition and formation of the subject.

In spite of this, however, fear manages somehow to tie itself around the dreaded object, though there occurs no dissecting or analyzing intention of so-being of the sort that would be characteristic of disgust. Hence, in spite of the paradox of disgust, its intentional structure shows itself to be the more uniform and self-contained of the two, and especially when we observe the relatively far-reaching unity of physical and moral disgust we may in consequence hope to penetrate more deeply into the essential nature of disgust through a phenomenological analysis of its objects.

III. The Disgusting

III.1. *The Senses and Disgust*

The main carriers of the sensation of disgust are the olfactory, visual, and tactile senses. As we know, the sense of taste can be reduced, from our present point of view, to the sense of smell, of which four fundamental differentia are recognized: sour, sweet, bitter, salt. There is in fact hardly a single disgusting taste that could not unmistakably be related to the corresponding odor. The bitter, sweetish, sour tonality of the related disgust sensation can however be further specialized. Smell and taste remain in any case intimately bound together, the sense of taste being absorbed by that of smell more often than the converse because—quite apart from any physiological consideration—the sense of smell, purely empirically, embraces an incomparably wider class of objects and is more readily regarded as a 'sense' in a narrower understanding, that is, as an object-giving function. There certainly exists a quite special relation between disgust and the quality of sweetness. One could not simply say that sweetness as such is disgusting, nor even that it is represented to a higher degree in disgusting taste configurations than are other basic tastes. (This may indeed be so in the case of bitterness.) Disgust at a sweet taste—an experience which is completely dependent on the detailed circumstances involved in the consumption of the dish in question, on associative elements—presupposes, somehow, an awareness of the image of what is conceived as being 'sweetish' or 'sugary'; it represents disgust of a 'higher order', and we shall indeed find it proper to consider it again briefly in the section on moral disgust.

What is more difficult to conceive, ignoring more or less subtle exceptions, is an experience of aural disgust. This is to be explained by the fact that hearing lacks any substantial intentionality, that it is detached from its objects; sounds and noises merely betray the existence of objects, they do not 'present' them in the sense in which this can be said of visual, tactile and olfactory sensations. Seeing, touching, and smelling grasp material objects from various different sides, each of them suffering under an essential limitation which cannot be transcended, but each possessing a kind of immediacy that is alien to the sense of hearing. Shape and color, surface and consistency, smell and taste contribute to an incomparably greater extent to the constitution of perceived objects than does their 'voice', the noises that they engender. It is as if the sound only acquires its 'origin', as it were, from the object that engenders it and thereafter constitutes an essence, perhaps even a world, of its own. It is from this that the sense of hearing acquires its 'analytical' character (because of its remoteness from the object-nexus), together with the possibility of a non-intentional sense-cosmos in the world of sounds, the possibility of 'pure music'. Even a fear of sounds exists only to a very modest degree. Fear of something dangerous that is communicated by verbal communication is as little aural fear as disgust at a printed pornographic story is disgust at what is seen. Even such a perfect example of aural fear as fear of thunder or of a threatening roar presupposes the thought of the origin of these phenomena and of a possible danger deriving from them to an even greater extent than in cases of fear at some threatening sight. The exceptions mentioned above might include disgust at sugary or sensual music, at a particular ugly voice, or at a chafing noise. But how far is what is disgusting in a lascivious whisper or in the rustle of a piece of paper crawled over by vermin really something that is disgusting for the ear? Not certainly in the sense in which the ear likes to hear praise, but in the sense in which it enjoys hearing concord. A cacophony is as little disgusting as is a chaotic pattern of colors, and there is nothing corresponding to visible disgusting objects in the realm of what is heard. All aural disgust is to a considerable extent 'moral disgust'; it presupposes a sufficiency of associations called forth in succession by the objects which in visual disgust are consigned to a far greater extent to the background of the intention. When I find a certain kind of beery bass voice disgusting, it makes me think vividly of the moral disgustingness of drunkenness, of unclean breath, and so forth; the sound of chewing and lip-smacking conjures up an optical portrait of greed and gluttony. When I find a seductive melody disgusting then the sensation I experience is vividly colored by the feeling that it is *I* who am being disgusted, that it is genuinely disgusting, that it is *so* disgusting, that in my present mood I find it disgusting, and so forth. One would search in vain for any even approximately equivalent parallel in the aural sphere to something like a putrid smell, the feel of a flabby body, or of a belly ripped open.

But even smell, sight, and touch do not support disgust in equal degree. For the true place of origin of disgust is the sense of smell. Disgusting smell-types present more solid unities and are less in need of associative appendages than other disgusting formations. Through the sense of smell (always including moments derived from the sense of taste, which partly intensify, partly restrict the whole) the upper digestive tract is in the most direct way affected, vomiting most often provoked, the moment of proximity most strongly brought to bear. Also through the organ of smell small particles of the alien object become incorporated into the subject, which makes an intimate grasping of the alien object [*Sosein*] possible. It is in the *intimacy* made possible by the sense of smell that there is rooted its primary significance for disgust, and this belongs together also with the urge which itself reflects back to the experience of eating. Here already attention may be drawn to the interconnections between disgust, smell, putrescence, decay, secretion, life, nourishment. Here we have a range of interconnections among intentions of various kinds which is entirely lacking in the case of fear, and which also in the case of hate does not exist in such a naturalistically definable form. (Compare the fundamental intentional character: a general disgusting so-being.)

In the second place, it seems clear that the tactile sense should follow; touch too is more intimate than sight, in a certain respect involving the moment of proximity in an even more accentuated form—though never suggesting such a high degree of intimacy as does the sense of smell. One need only think of the motif of being in contact with the disgusting object, of its pressing itself upon one, even of its adhering to one's own body. But still there are no longer here such unequivocal, crude tonalities of disgust as are to be found among the olfactory modes. It already requires a certain perversity to be able to ignore completely the disgusting character of putrescence and to acquire a taste for dubious kinds of food; but does anyone really need to overcome a feeling of disgust in order to acquire a taste for aspic, jellied fruits, purées, and so forth? And yet the tactile impression of flabbiness, sliminess, pastiness, and indeed of everything soft, should count among the disgusting. Or rather, these exhibit a predisposition for becoming disgusting.

For the sense of touch we already need to acknowledge a certain additional complexity, there being present new determining elements. This will be evident from the fact that the prototype of all disgusting objects seems to lie in putrefaction: think of the disgust arising through touching, say, pus, festering wounds, or putrid flesh become soft. There is one specific massive smell-complex of putrefaction, which, however indirectly, has the characteristic tactile consistency of decomposing organisms. Finally the physical contiguity of touch points in the direction of the second principal domain of intimate union after that of nourishment: sexuality, which indeed supplies us with an imposing number of disgust-moments. That the connection of sexuality with disgust is a looser one, or at least less prototypical, will be discussed later. For the present we note only that sexual rejection cannot be presented as any kind of analogue of vomiting in its specific functional character. (The idea of intimate contact with extraneous living substance is a central element in sexuality: compare the discussion of besmirching below.)

It is different again in the case of visual disgust. The sense of sight presents its object in a different way from the senses of touch or smell. On the one hand it can give an incomparably more many-sided, encompassing, and adequate image of the object—'seeing' something implies 'knowing' it in an entirely different sense from 'smelling' or 'touching' it. A single visual impression, a simple optical impression, does not, on the other hand, lead us into a region where we can grasp the essence of the object, as does an odor or a tactile sensation. For just as there exists a close relationship between seeing and discursive knowing, so also there exists a relation between smelling and touching and that kind of 'detecting' or 'feeling' an object which may, while dull and one-sided, and 'irresponsible' in relation to the object as a whole, still reach deeply enough. (Touching here bears more similarity to seeing than does smelling.) Put differently: visual sensation presents its object rather in a fully-constituted, fully formed manifoldness, together with all its colors, lines, perspectives etc., or certainly with some of these—this at least is its most prominent function. That a line or color may already say a great deal points either to a marginal case or to a shortened figure of speech: a *new* line (or color) may tell us much, but then only within some multiplicity with which we are already familiar. Either that, or it is a matter of purely deductive extrapolation: a red lantern shining at night may indicate to me an entire railway train (without presenting its features at all, not even in the roughest form). Phenomena which are already more expressive of an essential underlying nature are for example a sudden reddening (a blush) or a slim line. But, reverting to disgust, there are indeed also colors and appearance-qualities that are in general characteristic of putrefaction; they are however far less accentuated and unequivocal than in the case of odors or even tactile impressions. For the associative element, perhaps even the deductive ('syllogistic') element is represented here in a far more pointed way. Nevertheless there does exist here a further total quality of the appropriate kind and therefore also a genuine visual disgust; only the latter is founded more in other modalities of disgust than conversely. The formation (and perhaps also the cultivation) of disgust sensations are also genetically tied to smell, as also to the tactile sense, and only then—in due course—to the visual sense.

All of which can be formulated thus: the olfactory sense is the proper organ of disgust in virtue of its primacy. It is the organ of an 'intimate grasping of so-being'. But the visual sense has such a comprehensive grasp of the features of the object that in spite of its inadequacy in regard to intimacy it is able 'at first blow' to present a *sui generis* quality of disgust, which is again oriented, through the determination of its content, around the more primary olfactory disgust-quality.

If, furthermore, the linkage between the object-range of putrefaction is already looser in tactile disgust than in case of olfactory disgust, it is loosened still more in the case of visual disgust. There is in fact one relatively simple visual quality of the disgusting which already has very little (though still some residual) connection with putrefaction: the visual impression made by the pullulation of swarms of creeping insects. However, we cannot speak here of the kind of absolute disgustingness such as was found in the smell of putrefaction. For the visual disgust in question depends so much on the particular constitution of the creatures involved. What is significant is that the sense of sight seems to come into consideration as disgust-sense primarily where the object appears essentially as plurality and gives rise to disgust precisely through this aspect.

III.2. *Types of Physically Disgusting Objects*

In this section we shall present a survey of the typical objects of that kind of disgust whose central feature is that it is conveyed through immediate sense impressions, bypassing now any systematic investigation of the different roles played by the individual sense organs. We cannot avoid here a certain 'wallowing in filth', which unquestionably comes packaged with the given theme; we hope only that it will prove justified by its scientific interest, and our endeavor will be to reduce it to an absolute minimum. We may select, empirically, nine principal types of object:

a) The prototypical object of disgust is, as already intimated, the range of phenomena associated with putrefaction. This includes corruption of living bodies, decomposition, dissolution, the odor of corpses, in general the transition of the living into the state of death. Not however this state itself, since the non-organic is, in contrast, not at all experienced as disgusting. Not even a skeleton or a mummified corpse—for what is 'gruesome' is not 'disgusting'. The mark of a disgusting object is found quite specifically in the process of putrescence, and in its carrier. There exists an image of putrefaction as an optical-tactile-olfactory formation which is, although complicated, still such as to possess structural unity. Between, say, rotten meat and rotten fruit there is after all a similarity of coloration, not to speak of other common features such as softening. In general we repeat once more that something dead is never disgusting in its *mere non-functioning*, for then even fresh meat would be disgusting, which is definitely not the case. Rather, substantial decomposition is necessary, which must at least seem to put itself forward as a continuing process, almost as if it were after all just another manifestation of life. Already here we encounter the relation of disgust to what is positively vital, to what is animated. And indeed there is undoubtedly associated with the extinction of life in putrefaction a certain—quite remarkable—augmentation of life: a heightened announcement of the fact that life *is there*. Evidence of this is provided by the reinforced smell that accompanies putrefaction, the often glaring change of colors, the putrefied 'sheen', the whole phenomenon of turbulence characteristic of putrefaction. But not every pathologically intensified activity is disgusting: neither the ravings of a lunatic, nor the agony of the dying are so. It is not the living being as a whole that in dying becomes disgusting, but much more the body, in its parts: its 'flesh' for example. Thus it is not similarity to death in any sense that is disgusting, and neither is it the approach or moment of death—but rather the terminating section of life *in death*.

b) The disgustingness of excrement is also connected with its direction towards dissolution of concrete living material. These disintegrated by-products of life which are excreted from the body are in general disgusting. Certainly here is present what is merely a special case of putrefaction itself, for it is not at all the case that excreta are the most typical carriers of putrefaction, which can indeed even be absent from them. Quite apart from the connection with putrefaction, we have to deal here with a quite peculiar kind of transformation of living into dead matter. And this is again a manifestation of life, a concomitant of vital processes. Disgust is related therewith also to the character of excreta as waste products, to the circumstance that decomposed organic material indicates existence, or past existence, of life. For in the decomposition-products of life not only the withering of life but also the presence of life itself has a disgusting effect.

c) We have to distinguish from the above the disgusting character of bodily secretions. This involves a further move from the region of putrefaction, and therewith also the decisive role of odor is diminished. The demarcations between excreta and secreta are certainly, as it were, 'fluid'—the former are bare dross, the latter serve a specific function and thus are essentially free from putrefaction. Aside from the clear cases there are also a number of intermediate stages. In suppuration and similar processes the moment of putrefaction plays its part once more, and in a quite peculiar variant form: rottenness in a living body has it own special note of the disgustingly gruesome. For this kind of putrescence, though it too is occurrent and 'advancing', partakes also in a constancy, indeed it has a kind of eternal quality, which is absent in the putrefaction of stuff left to itself (of corpses, refuse, and the like). But the disgustingness of normal secretions is generally known. Its analysis is not quite trivial: the simple motif of 'substantial life coming to an end' would not yield an adequate account, even where it may be applicable at all. Much more it is primarily a matter of the general disgustingness of the viscous, semi-fluid, obtrusively clinging. The substances here alluded to (mucus, and so forth), as far as they force themselves upon our attention—something which always signifies, or at least suggests the possibility of an abnormal situation—carry the motif of an 'indecent surplus of life'—an abundance that, true to nature, points once more to death and to putrefaction, towards life which is in decline.

d) The types of disgust just alluded to—disgust toward what is viscous, what adheres in an improper place—manifests itself also more generally in a manner less specifically bound up with specific materials. We have noticed already that everything disgusting, conceived purely intentionally, somehow 'adheres' to the subject, embraces it with its proximity, with its miasma, (though not necessarily, as it were, catching it in a net from which there is no escape). This expresses itself in particular in the phenomenon of dirt. As far as we can see, dirt is the only typical object of disgust that is not closely connected to decaying life or indeed to any kind of life. For my hand is still dirty even when it is merely covered with, say, soot or dust, and it would then be unappetizing to touch food with, or—where this is permitted—somebody's face. On closer inspection however this too proves to be less simple. For what exactly is dirt? The moment of harmfulness is here certainly not a central one; it is a quite secondary awareness that eating with unwashed hands may have effects harmful to one's health. We would not, after all, shrink away from a hand that has been dipped into, say, cholera germs as from one which were merely dirty. Indeed it precisely belongs to the essence of dirt that it presents a relative harmlessness, merely some kind of vague noxiousness. But this does not contain its essential nature, for we would not honor a toadstool, for example, that looks just a trifle suspicious, with the epithet of being 'dirty'. On the other hand it would be inadequate to define dirt as 'a thing which is located at an improper place'. For should I find precious stones scattered in a peat bog, I would not say that the peat were 'filthy with diamonds', but much rather that I had found diamonds in a heap of dirt. Even a sooty hand is not a characteristically dirty hand. We think of dirt more readily as a grayish black layer of uncertain composition, above all as involving smallish sticky particles of which this stickiness is more essential than is the stuff from which they originate. There exists here a substantial connection with feces (though how far physiological reminiscences play a role here is left for another time), and also with grease and sweat. But this much is correct in the definition of dirt rejected above, for it appears in fact, that it makes itself felt as a phenomenon in those places where it does not belong, where its effect is disturbing and disfiguring, where it has somehow made a home for itself to the extent that it cannot simply be shaken off. Such places are surfaces of the body or articles generally found in close contact with the body. And here is after all revealed an unmistakable intentional relation to life, and to life's ebbs and flows. Hands become dirty through manual activity, underclothes through being worn. And there is often sweat that plays an agglutinating role in the formation of dirt. Dirt is, to an extent, simply the presence, the non-obliteration, of traces of life. This may be either, in a purely formal way, a bare indication of the fact, or by the medium of a 'material' (precisely that black-grayish something), which is a quite specific phenomenon and in no sense one of the compact well-characterized 'vital substances' (secretions, and so on.). While therefore, the moment of disgust presented by dirt is in regard to content a rather minimal one, nevertheless the formal traits of adulteration, of shapelessness, and indeed of 'uncleanliness'—of an accentuated, virtually embodied negation of the idea of distance—reveals a quite unique disgust-inducing character. However, what is formally the principal feature of disgusting objects, their somehow obtrusive clinging-to-the-subject (to the one who is disgusted), and what gives rise to disgust through an inherent adherence, are two different things. We shall have to say more about their relationship in what follows. But when he or she becomes dirty the very phenomenon of adherence is brought home to the subject in a palpable way. This mushy mixture of particles without qualities attaches itself, as it comes into being, to the skin of human beings as they go about their activities.

e) We enter now an essentially different sphere: that of disgust-arousing *animals*, and in particular of *insects*. Here one may perhaps best speak most generally of *crawling animals* (vermin, invertebrates), which will serve also to indicate the principal motif of the disgust which is aroused. More highly organized animals rarely provoke any specific disgust, except perhaps as a result of an accidental uncleanliness, of their sometimes embarrassing smell, of their 'animalic warmth' which some people may find disgusting—all things which under certain circumstances may make even human beings disgusting. Whether the ritual prohibition of particular animals in certain religions were to any significant extent founded in genuine disgust (at the thought of eating them) would be difficult to decide.

There exists quite certainly a disgust aroused by animals of a sort which hardly needed to be encouraged by religious sanctions. And quite apart from this quantitative aspect of the matter, there is a kind of disgust which is in no way confined to the idea of eating but which relates directly to the sight, to the proximity of the creature in question. Many who would vehemently reject horsemeat nevertheless harbor great love for this noble companion of mankind. Note, however, that the disgust for worms, vermin, and other kinds of invertebrates does not belong to this category.

Among higher animals, it is the rat, in particular, that has to be mentioned. Against this mammal there is directed an almost universal feeling of specific disgust, frequently intertwined with a feeling of indefinable anxiety, of the uncanny. Some part may be played here by the fact that there is no other mammal which is, in its entire lifestyle, so vermin-like as the rat. Thus they are creatures with unattractively lithe, gray, elongated bodies, which appear in multitudes, lurk in dark crannies, exhibit parasitic tendencies and a dull, insidious character, and which call forth a relation to filth and to disease.

When we turn to snakes, here the associated disgust seems to be still more intermixed with anxiety (as of something sinister). Nearly everything that is disgusting in snakes—their slithering, creeping treacherousness, their chill activity—is present also in insects. As to vermin themselves, here too I do not wish to go into great detail. Differences of disgust-feelings between individuals are very considerable. In general, disgust is reduced to a low level or vanishes altogether for those insects with hard carapaces which do not form swarms; thus most beetles are not taken for disgusting. The same holds also of insects which fly rather than crawl (bees). What determines the disgust aroused by vermin is, in general, an interaction of several factors, some of which may indeed be partly lacking in particular less pronounced cases. These are: their crawling stickiness, their appearance of being as it were 'pasted over' their substrate (which is more pronounced in the case of certain bugs in virtue of their flat bodies); their pullulating squirming, their cohesion into a homogeneous teeming mass; their evocation—partly apparent, partly real—of decomposition and decay. What is real is a frequent preference for putrescent organic material; what is apparent—without thereby necessarily being of no significance—is the impression that they themselves are somehow part of such stuff, as if they had

originated from it, as if their frantic teeming activity were a phenomenon of life in decay. Altogether it is in general the strange cold-
ness, the restless, nervous, squirming, twitching vitality which they
exhibit—as if it were all somehow an abstract demonstrative dance
of life without however any appropriate feelings of warmth and
without inner substance of life. Finally, however, there is the insidious, aggressive character that is to be found in most of these creatures. The role of the latter has often been overestimated; it has
become customary to suppose that disgust towards insects is perhaps
only a phylogenetically inbred form of anxiety or fear. But this does
not capture the essence of the matter: for while such fear may be
present, even such that it does not fully come to consciousness, it is
yet something which can only be a supplement to disgust, far from
something which might engender it. Disgust relates less to the
objective danger provoked by these creatures in particular circumstances—we are, after all, able to experience a fear of bees and wasps
which is honestly and quite generally free of disgust—than to their
quality (anchored only secondarily in their *Dasein*) of being malicious, their hidden malevolence, this quite peculiar mixture of sly
furtiveness and demonstrative, impertinent activity, of futility with
eager, stinging fervor. Even if disgust may fulfill the teleological
function of a warning, this as little captures the intentional significance of disgust as it would the sensation of erotic-aesthetic attraction, on the grounds that there are those who avoid contact with
strikingly beautiful women with an instinctive circumspection. To
sum up, there is hardly anything more to say than that disgusting
creatures arouse generally the impression of life caught up in a senseless, formless surging, that they somehow urge themselves upon the
subject with a life-corroding breath of moldiness of decay which can
be concretely perceived. The particular severity and force of this
kind of disgust derives from the fact of the mobility and aggressiveness of the object (not however from its dangerousness), from the
consciousness that contact with it could so easily come about. Also,
the possibility of a phylogenetically suppressed desire to use insects
as nourishment may be involved. Disgust would then be intensified
through the nervous defense reaction against such a desire. Also the
general desire that may arise in us to crush this disgusting thing may
serve only to intensify further the accent of disgust in the associated
intuitive content.

f) In reference to foods we must immediately make the following important distinction. Foods are not things that simply come
our way; they are functionally integrated into our lives as material
that we are to consume. It is quite different if they cause disgust precisely in this capacity rather than merely as things, as bare material.
The latter is the case in regard to foods that have been spoiled; it
would be disgusting to keep such in my room, even though there
would clearly be no question of my eating them. But it may also be
the case for example with regard to foods towards which someone
may have a powerful specific aversion; when he cannot stand the
smell of onions, say, or the sight of gravy. There exists indeed a quite
general, though slight, disgust aroused by leftovers and by plates
that are covered with them. A second group of cases however
involves disgust that arises only when, for some external reason, a
particular food should actually be consumed. It may happen that
somebody does not mind a jug of milk standing on his table the
whole day through, but that he loses control over his stomach
immediately when he tries to take a drink from it. The case is similar when one experiences temporary aversion against dishes that one
has otherwise enjoyed.

The first group of cases here is connected with disgust aroused
by putrefaction, or by a sticky, dirty mishmash (compare also the disgust aroused by unsuitable combinations of foods). The second
group involves partly a reference towards those elements of disgust
which relate to the preservation of life and of its functioning, partly
to the more abstract, formal and in this sense 'moral' disgust
aroused by satiety. Thus we can see that there is no uniformly comprehensible type of disgust relating to foods. This is because, even
taking into account the various typical cases, individual differences
are here too great. In virtue of the close links with both mouth and
stomach, all aversions relating to foods appear here in the form of
disgust. This applies, for example, in the reluctance arising through
the unfamiliarity of a certain food, where the unfamiliarity of, say, a
landscape will of course not be met with feelings of disgust.
However, the customary attempts to explain the idiosyncrasies of
tastes in foods—that somebody abhors a dish because he is accustomed not to eat it, or because it had on one occasion upset his
stomach—are rather shallow and inadequate. It should in general be
kept in mind that in regard to most kinds of food there is an inher-

ent possibility for disgust on the strength of its very claim to be consumed; its sticky, moist, somehow soiled condition, its associations with past events of the most varied kind, or, finally, the real or apparent reference to a putrefaction which is often present. Furthermore, it can even be the case that a dish may be disgusting as a *thing* when as food it is not disgusting. This is indeed a quite general matter, and harmless as long as it is merely a question of the smell of fresh food or some other accentuated smell characteristic of food occurring outside mealtimes, but which may clearly have a disturbing, even some kind of disgusting effect—as of course, may everything in this sensory sphere which intrudes upon us at the wrong time.

There exists also the perverse type of preference for slightly putrescent tastes, namely the *haut-goût* of roast game. The Chinese were said to prefer completely rotten eggs, something which I would credit less to the 'differences of taste' which are so much overestimated by foolish relativists, then to a passion for esoteric refinement on the part of an extraordinarily overcultivated civilization. Whether the disgustingness of rotten eggs is intentionally apparent to the Chinese as the disgustingness of rotten meat is to the lovers of *faisandé*, I do not know: the states of consciousness may well be here somehow different. (The inclination towards the excessively bizarre seems again to be characterized by what is in the end a kind of shallow naiveté.) A more widespread case, and one which is still more harmless as no meat is involved, is that of penetratingly smelly cheeses, which undoubtedly contain something that has to be recognized as putrefaction. Most persons who like to eat cheese are still prepared to admit that they may find its odor disgusting, that it would perhaps induce them to pull their faces outside of mealtimes. Obviously we have here a case of a delicately equivocal evaluation, what one might call an eroticism of disgust which can take hold in a particular restricted sphere. (Restricted license of a similar kind as something which is both extraordinary and yet free of sanction—although of accentuated vitality—exists also in other contexts: for example the erotic freedom which may arise through dancing in otherwise 'decent' society. Or, to remain in the gastronomic sphere, think of how much one likes to drink beer even though its taste is really rather bad! It is simply something that is to be drunk and not—as in the case of wine—to be tasted and enjoyed and as it were examined intensively and evaluatively.)

(g) The human body in proximity can also by itself arouse disgust. One would generally explain this phenomenon as pathological, as a type of hysteria—except that it involves conditions or peculiarities of the body or bodily products that are acknowledged to be disgusting in themselves, in particular when this phenomenon represents something typical. Moreover bodily aroused disgust is undoubtedly to be found in the spectrum of emotions even of healthy beings. The disgust which a healthy person feels against, for instance, homosexual advances, is certainly not directed only against the idea of sexual inversion, but also against the alien body itself, which is conceived as the agent in the attempt. Disgust may also be aroused by the embrace of a radically unloved person of the opposite sex. Or, still more harmlessly: how many persons are seized by a modicum of disgust when they are penned together with others in a tram or bus, or when they have to take a seat which is still warm from its previous occupant? There exists indeed a quite normal propensity towards bodily disgust, which exerts itself, admittedly only in specific circumstances—such as, for example, where the body obtrudes upon us simply as such, when it makes itself felt too much *as a body*, so that it is devoid of that 'human' role which makes it acceptable. The disgust which is meant here certainly contains also a reference to the sexual sphere, in particular to the possibility of a general absence of inhibition and restraint, of a formlessness which is unavoidably suggested by an unaccustomed or, more precisely, unmotivated bodily intimacy which, at least for the subject involved, serves no function. But this kind of disgust can select the alien body as its intuitive object only, because the body can serve as a collecting agent for disgust-tonalities of other kinds, which have already been referred to. Generally valid is the disgust aroused by the inside of the body, including human blood, when this becomes perceptible. It is then however mingled with horror, anxiety, perturbation. It does not seem necessary to offer here a special explanation of the association of the exposed interior of the body and of every conspicuous lack of covering, with decay, putrescence, disorderly exposure of vital phenomena, the fouling up of life.

(h) Something else which we may be permitted to mention as physical disgust, another tendency which although often recurring, yet shades off into the pathological, is the disgust aroused by exuberant, exaggerated fertility. As this was bravely expressed by Otto

Weininger,[6] someone who indeed cannot be absolved of Manichaean error: "All fecundity is simply disgusting." Perhaps however being disgusted by the sight of swelling breasts, by swarming broods of some species of animal, fish-spawn, perhaps even by rank, overgrown vegetation, is something which is not known exclusively to psychopaths out of touch with reality, even though it may only be in such cases that it is decisive in their feeling of life. One need think only of the association with vermin, or of what is mentally disgusting in the idea of formless effervescence of life, of interminable directionless sprouting and breeding, which then points so inescapably to the idea of rapid decay on a massive scale.

(i) Finally we refer to the disgust aroused by disease and by bodily deformation. This has been already elucidated to some degree in our remarks on excretion and secretion, putrefaction, and the body and its interior. What we are dealing with here is an unfamiliar and exaggerated living growth (a tumor, an ulceration, an abscess) which at the same time is already shading off into decomposition. The allusion to the death of the total organism clearly calls forth in the first place more horror than disgust; yet the more concrete and vivid the horror, the more it inclines towards disgust. In the case of cripples it is not the functional inadequacy which has a disgusting effect—the latter never arises, for example, in cases of deafness, nor of limping—but the deformation of shape, since every defect in a visible part of the body somehow determines also some additional positive feature, such as a bloody stump. Thus it is not the mere imperfection of life in itself, but rather the *life in the wrong place* that is perhaps founded therein—the precipitous slope of life in its plasticity—which evokes disgust. It seems indeed above all the intensified (not simply 'mechanized') activity of life which is disgusting in its exaggerated operation, insofar as this exceeds the limits of a real, or as it were quasi-'personal', purposeful organic unity.

III.3. *Types of Morally Disgusting Objects*

By 'moral' here we understand not 'ethical' in a strict and narrow sense, but rather: mental or spiritual [*geistig*], albeit more or less with reference to ethical matters, in contrast to physical, as when one speaks of moral factors or of the morally relevant aspect of an issue. An attempt at a classification of the disgust tonalities now under consideration can lay even less claim to be based on secure evidence than our classification of the rather more clear-cut types of object arousing physical disgust. Here we shall distinguish five types:

(a) If the material involved is of an appropriate character then the feeling of displeasure that is evoked by tiresome monotony can acquire a tinge of disgust (the disgust aroused by satiety). Satiety in the strict sense comes about only when a constantly repeated experience had been originally or is in normal circumstances a pleasurable one; it is then not only the object but also our enjoyment of it that becomes disgusting. (When I say that I have at last grown weary of some torment, this has nothing in common with authentic satiety; it means simply: 'I have lost my patience'. Just as one sometimes says 'enough of this joke!' or: 'I can take it no longer'.) We can see here again the relation of disgust to a one-sidedly exaggerated kind of life, one that is as it were endlessly oscillating within an enclosed space. A feeling of disgust holds us back, one might say, from drowning in pleasure. One cannot say that what we have here is simply a pleasure that has ceased to be pleasurable; rather, that the pleasure involved becomes merely shallow, barren, reduced to a state where it is in perceptible contrast with the will to life of the person. Here it need not necessarily be a matter of a particular pronounced type of pleasure. It is not the object itself that is important. Rather it is the fact that it persistently endures which gives rise to a defense reaction. The object is then pleasurable to the extent that everything else that is experienced is of itself and other things being equal also enjoyable, as having an accent that stands positive to life.

More typical forms of satiety however attach themselves to what is pleasurable in the more narrow sense. This belongs to that sort of disgust which arises when one thinks back to a recently surmounted state of intoxication (and not only just of an alcoholic kind); not because each such state lasts for an endless time, but rather because it contains so overwhelming and stomach-turning a concentration of enjoyment. A similar type of disgust can follow as a consequence of any enjoyment which, even though not itself a kind of intoxication, is yet sufficiently concentrated and closed in upon itself to stand out from the rest of life as a recurrent special delicacy, as when one has been served daily with a specific kind of biscuit, or when one becomes, after a long period, overwhelmed with the pleasures of the table, or when one has rested in bed for too long. It is characteristic of such conditions of satiety—as distinct from mere boredom—that one experiences a certain loss of the sense of time, a feeling of time-lessness, of being turned in upon oneself, of sterility, of an endless and ever-increasing condition of self-satiation, a kind of giddiness, a disorientation of one's life and a feeling of entering an almost celes-tial realm from which one would wish finally to return to a drier and more invigorating air. This holds of every kind of pleasurable dally-ing which has at last become aimless and perhaps also for certain other specific conditions. Even perhaps, when these are bound up with enduring inactivity, health, and well-being, they can for most human beings, become disgusting in this sense. (Compare the dis-solution in the style of Oblomov in Goncharov's novel, which indeed was in the end also unhealthy, even physically deadly, but which was in its origin rooted in a quite robust and not at all ner-vous state of good health.) In the gastronomic sphere it is sweets, above all, that can most easily become disgusting, since it is just the moment of sweetness that forms the basic tonality of what one might call a self-consistent, undemarcated and formless, insipidly agreeable taste. (A profound analysis of the significance of tastes would be an undertaking of some attraction, but is out of place here.)

Finally, the disgust of satiation has certainly something in com-mon with the specific disgust that we feel towards incest, either between brother and sister or still more between parent and child. Aristotle has expressed this somewhat clumsily as follows: that a fusion of the two most powerful kinds of tendernesses towards one and the same person would be highly 'inexpedient'. There is some-thing extraordinarily shallow, a horrifyingly sickly-sweet desolateness in the idea that the primordial, childlike communion of the family (and of mother and child before birth) should be burdened also with sexual life: an example of a constricting blockage of the stream of life. Thus disgust at the idea of incest may be explained at least in part as a type of satiation. (It should be added that the matter of the immorality of incest is not even touched by this, let alone exhausted.—Perhaps all this may be applied with a grain of salt also to marriage. But one should not forget: 1. That in marriage monot-ony is something vitally significant; that it is, at least in principle, purposefully directed and is not a mere capsule of self-indulgence, the possibility of which I hold in fact to be one ethical danger of monogamous erotic relations. 2. That the normal relation of marriage by no means engenders a 'family community' in the same sense as does such a relationship of blood and common extraction, to which sexual communion then can be added through incest. Incest sexualizes and reabsorbs life, marriage validates sexuality and is a foundation of life.)

(b) The next object of moral disgust is excessive vitality or vitality whose unfurling is misplaced. This can arouse disgust only under the presupposition that it can force itself into a certain *proximity* with the subject in such a way as to threaten substantially to sweep along with the latter's vitality; the disgusting effect is usually conditioned also by a trait of this excessive vitality that is somehow life-betraying and suggestive of decay in the widest sense. When, for example, somebody is very strong and executes extraordinary physical feats, this can hardly bring on the effect of disgust. This is perhaps more likely if he is a pronouncedly muscular type with a spiritual life that is entirely neglected; the impression of a debauchery of life may then more likely arise, together with the doubtfulness as to the vital value of the whole. Brutality, physical energy blustering in all directions, a concentrated odor of life, may occasionally be disgusting, even though never motivating the typical disgust reaction. This will be the case the more that the given phenomena are charged with an element of aggressiveness, coerciveness, insidiousness, of the sort that is precisely indispensable for producing disgust. Every disgusting reaction contains an element of plain resistance, and this is first of all the vehement *rejection of a presumption*. It is not only that the release which is the reaction of disgust becomes actualized by the spatial proximity of the object which provokes it; the object itself requires, in order to be disgusting, that a proximizing tendency be represented in its so-being, a moment of nearness which also carries with it a tendency to encroach within the orbit of experience of the perceiving (knowing) subject. It is in the fulfillment of this condition that there is rooted the very extensive disgust-arousing capacity of disordered sexuality. We find completely fused therein the moment of a vitality that surges and smolders in itself: the accentuation of the moment of proximity, and the urge towards the transference of this proximity into the sphere of experience of the affected subject. To this must be added the fact that the sexual instinct is, as is well known, one of the most important basic living drives, directed towards a certain quite general goal of life. At the same time however—for profound biological and metaphysical reasons which cannot be argued further here—this instinct cannot be activated purely mechanically. Rather, in its fulfilment and also in the first partial steps thereto it issues forth in a series of associated formations which are more or less independent and this in a broad way involving all sorts of extensions and transformations. There is hardly a single element in our lives which sexuality does not attempt to press into its service or at least affects in some way, grasping or marking it. The ethical question as to when this must be recognized and inhibited as morally evil or still just as 'irregular' does not fall within the scope of this essay; in general one should think here of perverse, polygamic sexuality, of an order which is inimical to life or which is overwhelming. There is here a vast realm of objects of disgust, though it should be mentioned immediately that disgust and ethical censure do not run strictly in parallel with each other, disgust being on the one hand directed to specific aspects and types of sexual immorality, and on the other hand capable of being felt without the accompanying properly ethical judgment which should follow in its wake. The disgust reaction will be directed against the immoral to the extent that the latter is experienced as a 'soiling', a 'sullying' of life and its values, and, to a somewhat lesser degree, perhaps, against a 'satanic' or mechanical and superficial sexuality. (We might compare here also the distinction between disgust and contempt in Section IV.1 below.) But further, even the presentation of sexual behavior that is not strictly sinful can arouse disgust, either through accidental proximity or for its harmless lack of taste, as more sensitive persons can be affected by public references to the wedding night at a wedding banquet. In fact anything with a sexual accent can easily come to have a disgusting effect on the majority of persons. This is almost always the case when, despite an initial invitation, sexual attraction or excitement fails to come to realization; here one may also oscillate between attraction and disgust. (It is indeed 'abnormal' if the feeling of disgust here is blunted or hypertrophied, or also tolerated as a regular combination with other sexual excitations.)

We can ask at this stage why the paradigmatic disgust reaction complex should have its seat not in the sexual but in the gastric region. The reason for this lies partly in the greater simplicity and unequivocality of the relationships which hold in the latter region, but still more in the location of the vomiting-reaction, the antiperistaltically-induced 'no!' motion, an analogue of which in the sexual sphere is entirely absent. (This again is obviously connected with the fact that sexual union, quite apart from the duality of roles, knows no counterpart of the imbibing, incorporating of food which takes place in eating.) Thus, disordered sexuality represents for the sense of disgust, above all what is disorderly, unclean, clammy, the unhealthy excess of life. Even spirituality in the wrong place may to the best of our knowledge arouse something like disgust. There is something disgusting in the idea of everything on earth becoming pasted over with musings and broodings, or with hair-splitting calculations. The fruitlessness of ceaseless cerebration as an end in itself, the consequent obstruction of the course of life, and indeed also of thought must bring a feeling of shallowness that is indubitably related to disgust. If a soldier responds to a command of his superior with an investigation of its correctness, and in other such cases of misplaced criticism and intellectual flabbiness, these will often be felt to be not only improper and absurd or pernicious, but also to be disgusting. And so, too, will that type of aimless and over-subtle intellectual activity, better termed intellectual *wantonness*, that kind of subjective, irresponsible, and opulent, over-refined and sometimes bombastic reveling in thought itself and in its exhibition, which is at heart indifferent to its object: what one might call lascivious intellectualism. (A good means of familiarizing oneself with this is through the atmosphere of Thomas Mann's novel *The Magic Mountain*.) Or we may call it: spirituality, over-clever intellectuality without rigor and backbone (the disgusting trait of journalism), where a flickering and steaming of the mind darkens and suffocates the intentional reference, the will to speak in a straightforward way. Whether everyone would confirm an experience of disgust in this regard is rather doubtful. But there is a more generally manifested disgust precisely against the overintellectualized tearing into sexual matters, which is seen in opposition to straightforward compulsion as having a certain sordidness. This is, to be sure, a matter of the prevailing intention: intellectual elaboration in whatever sphere, including that of sexuality, does not of itself signify anything that can be called sordid. It is merely that there exists here the danger that intellectual dallying and raking about may itself come to form a part of sexual life, on the strength of the enormous capacity for inflection and amalgamation with alien spheres which the sexual drive possesses (compare section IV.1). It belongs to the total disgust reaction that it is a matter of an essentially cumulative, infectious process, of something which lacks (also in a formal sense) restraint or hold, something which hones in on everything, something putrefied, and at the same time still undirected, undynamic, swirling about in its own dank atmosphere.

(c) The sphere of morally disgusting formation includes further the *lie*, the character trait of mendacity. Again we shall not seek to provide a complete ethical theory of the whole phenomenon of falsehood [*Unkorrektheit*], but shall concern ourselves only with its relation to disgust. The abhorrence that shoots through us when we ascertain that something is a lie seems to contain a constituent of disgust; but the element of disgust is more clearly represented in the repulsion which is manifested against a person known to be deceitful. Mendacity is neither the mere occurrence of lies, even less is it an inclination to self-deceit or to the pathological telling of lies. Rather, it is an inner indifference to truth and untruth, on the strength of which one may even deceive oneself, take no pains to achieve clarity, and even, in the presence of some substantial motive, assert falsehoods without a trace of inner disturbance. What bestows the accent of disgustingness upon lying is first of all what might be called a wormlike, crookedly hidden aggressiveness. I am seized already by a quite strong type of disgust when listening to, say, fawning, flattering speech that I know to be at bottom not well-intended. I have then before me something that is at least formally hostile, something that seeks to subdue me, which at the same time forces itself upon me—indeed forces itself into a proximity of a sort that is precluded for any kind of threatening violence. To this must now be added that side of the phenomenon of lying which does not concern immediately the person to whom the lie is told: the fact that a false statement is consciously made. We have here a penetration of the immediate concerns of life (be this a matter of someone's 'interest' in a tangible sense, or some kind of impulse or other vital motive) into the sphere of intentional activity, which ought to be the exclusive province of objective, purely factual determinateness and serve in precisely this sense the intellectual and vital concerns of life. Certainly deliberate false statements—as distinct from error—can exist only in regard to a hearer, however imaginary or abstract he may be. The hearer is, however, from this point of view a marginal factor only: as an intellectual formation the lie itself reveals the twisted, sodden modification of factual intention mentioned above; it is bloated with vital matter which is at odds with itself.

In the case of mendacity, now, this naturally expresses itself in a still more tangible, more substantial, somehow still more putrefied way. Here the person to whom the lie is told, as well as the immediately relevant motive, recede completely into the background. What comes to light in the foreground is the fact that—in contrast to what should be a matter of course and be called forth by the situation—the person concerned is not giving of himself. Where it ought to be possible to lay hold of him through the system of his material intentions, he is instead hidden by a layer of slimy, dirty vitality. To this must be added: 1. That this laying hold of or grasping of a person as a whole, in this or any other context, cannot and should not be anything other than a very incomplete one. But this does not affect at all either the demand or the possibility of material straightforwardness and open, non-deceitful frankness. 2. That further this particular disgusting trait, with certain deviations at the margin, also adheres only to the character of inner mendacity, and thus to the crooked, deceitful, cowardly, and thoroughly affect-loaded life of thought and conviction.

(d) Disgust at any kind of *falsehood*, infidelity, betrayal and so forth is to be judged similarly, and the various shades and differences of the degree of disgustingness of these phenomena need not further detain us. But it seems to me that one variety of incorrectness or fakeness would merit special mention, which can be designated in the widest sense as corruption. Human consciousness considers something 'dirty', and therefore as disgusting, when the manifold of life-values and particularly certain kinds of noble values are brought down to the level of monetary worth, as if they had been melted down to base metal. First there is a lie—and a falseness—here, for what we have to deal with is not any kind of sincerely intended universal economism (a thing of impossibility), but rather a simulation of values, valid in themselves, which are used only to mask monetary interests (such as the mask of unselfish public service where public life is corrupted). This does not yet serve to characterize the peculiar uncleanness of the phenomenon in question; it is much more a matter of the particular aptitude of money for uprooting other values and entrenching itself in their place. There surges up here involuntarily the image of a formless, homogeneously pappy, pulpy, carious mass which forces its way into the healthy tissue of a fully living manifoldness, replacing it with the corrosion of a life-imitating deadliness. But it is precisely in this that the feature essential to corruption is firmly based; the values which are repressed—honor, public welfare, conviction, and so on—do not simply disappear in order to make room for a homogeneous cosmos of monetary values (this would make way for something like a metaphysical collapse rather than corruption). It is, rather, that the repressed values live on, partly as mere masks, but partly also (because only then is corruption really possible) in a diminished and uprooted form, and also as real value-forces. It is in just this essential, apparently progressive dissolution and uprooting that there resides the putrefying aspect of corruption, the picture of a living substance in decay. Entirely in concordance with this is the fact that corruption also generally displays a luster of putrescence and semblance of flourishing, that it partakes of a certain quick-wittedness, a venturesomeness, a polymorphous manifold of surface qualities, novelties, and pseudo-values of many kinds which serve to conceal the musty omnipotence of mammon. Here too we are indubitably presented with a special kind of life surplus and the disgust that is directed against it has much in common with the disgust of surfeit, satiety, which has precisely a barren plentifulness as its object. It is worth mentioning also that the type of disgust dealt with here seems to be closely related to the disgust aroused by that which is *undignified*. Undignified is what is homogeneous, the crude, whatever is caught up restlessly in its own self-assertion and expansiveness—a boundless vitality without problems or ideals. But money too, the *nervus verum*, can become the basis of a similar crude life-monism, as can the original biological life-impulse. (The sociology of this phenomenon cannot be dealt with appropriately in the present framework.) It is however obvious why, in regard to mammonism, we feel less of the breath of physiological disgust and more the smell of dirt, and discern even in spite of a far reaching melding [*Verschmelzung*] with the most basic undignified, vulgar, raw interests of life—the atmosphere of the worm-eaten and of decay. These life-interests include under present social conditions also the basic biological needs, but in its general spirit and intention it does not signify simply the transference of the biological will to life into a 'civilized' sphere but rather a striving for the realization of a value which, even from the biological point of view, harbors in itself impoverishment and distortion.

(e) We conclude the present account with an indication of the disgust-reference of all *moral softness*, that is of inconstancy, flabbiness—weakness of character in the sense not so much of untruthfulness and infidelity as of a moral amorphousness, of an intrinsic, essential and unrestrained spinelessness. An inner incapability to adopt either a firm resolve or a sustained attitude of perseverance belongs more in this sphere than does, for example, cowardice proper, which is contemptible rather than disgusting since it presents us with no substantial intuitive image of the person involved. To this belong also sentimentality, moral stupor, and even dull-witted gushing and reveling, the whole range of insolidity of the intellectual and moral life. All of this can—though it need not—provoke in the observer a reaction of disgust. It resembles that type of disgust that is aroused by self-exalting luxuriation in spirituality, except that it relates not to the total arrangements and intentions of intellectual life in general, but rather to the more intimate formations bound up therewith, including all of its associated psychic emotions.

A disgust of this kind is experienced by many (myself included), at that exaltation of the soul and of feelings that characterizes a certain part of Russian literature and still more the world of ideas of some of its more sycophantic admirers. Here again it is the soft gushing type of life which resists all solid formations, all discrimination, selection, all following up towards a goal and towards significance, which has a disgusting effect as a result of the disparity between the scarcity of value-content which is involved and the stupefying exuberance of life. (In a more profound sense all of this bustle of the soul is of course also false and deceitful; for genuine strength of life and grandeur of soul will always manifest firmness, constancy and the will towards form, but still the individual emotions can exhibit genuineness and sincerity. The latter is more often to be found in Russian than in German advocates of the cult of 'the Russian soul'.) It is not without reason that all living material that as such makes itself too conspicuous only too easily becomes suspected of beginning a process of putrefaction. For it is a highly significant lesson of experience that a slight putrefaction still does not suppress the specific smell and taste of the material in question, but indeed accentuates them to an extent which makes them even more characteristic—the phenomenon of *haut goût*—thereby forcing to ever greater heights the peculiarly irrational vital content of that material. Only rarely will the experienced eye fail to detect associations of dissolution and uncleanness in the soul that exhibits a peculiarly intense-feeling life, a life dripping with "depth"—that is a life wherein the main accent is placed on feelings themselves and from which objective goals, even those which are most profound and difficult to formulate, are lacking.

III.4. *The Relation of Disgust to Life and Death*

We can draw the conclusion that disgust is provoked by the proximity or by the challenging or disturbing effect of certain formations which are constituted in such a way that they refer in a determinate manner to life and to death. What now are we to understand by this 'determinate manner' and what by 'challenge'?

(a) The surplus of life in disgusting formations signifies: accentuation, exaggerated representation, swollen overloadedness of vitality or of what is organic, as opposed to norm, direction, and plan of life, framework [*Gerüst*]—a word in which there is indicated the full significance to the individual life of the non-organic, of what is as it were schematically adumbrated. This surplus of life may be either a matter of some more or less exaggerated aspect of a still existentially coherent individual life (a gross, undignified, as it were perspiring, steaming impulse of life), or the *danse macabre* of living matter occasioned by the coming to an end of a real existence as a personal being: decay, repulsion, and the secretion of substance. There may also be differences in our answer to the question how far this phenomenon can be attributed metaphysical validity and how far it is supplemented or created by associative thinking on the part of the person concerned. Yet still, in the *phenomenon* of disgust this surplus of life is necessarily contained. In our opinion, and perhaps this can be supported by several previous statements, there is a metaphysical reality which corresponds to this phenomenon; the contrast between redundant oscillation of life and life which is structured by purpose is itself a metaphysical datum and not the product of some oversensitive imagination. Of course, in each individual concrete case, and also in relation to every type of disgust, the extent to which this imagination is involved may vary. It reaches its minimum, perhaps, in purely putrefactive disgust.

The life-exuberance which we have here designated as a disgust-motif is related to the lower rather than to those higher forms of life which are to a greater extent guided by the intellect. It relates also to coalescence in contrast to delimitation and individuality. For the less organized forms of life do indeed incline more towards uninhibited proliferation and luxuriant growth and reveal thereby an indifference to quality. Intellectual life always signifies tension, control, restraint, and proportion. Lower forms of life are in a certain way more naked; they are mere life, and only in this sense can they have anything to do with the moments of disgust. Corporeality, physical exuberance, robustness, earthiness do not belong at all in this sphere. It is neither rootedness in the lower sphere of being, nor these lower spheres themselves, which can become an object of disgust, but only a disordered, somehow pretentious inflatedness that is according to its intention unlimited. We do not use the word 'earthy' in relation to swarms of slithering, almost subterranean vermin as we do in relation to a certain type of human being—which is indeed quite the opposite type to what we think of as disgusting; such vermin evoke much rather the image of a patch of earth become agitated, enlivened in unseemly fashion. Voracious greed may be disgusting, but not for instance the preference for hearty substantial meals. The moments of adulteration and absence of differentiation make us think of putrefaction and of its limitless drive to extend and homogenize itself, or disgusting elements such as gangrenous moisture, pulpiness, clamminess, stickiness. The surplus life, in the sense here employed, endeavors to break altogether through any boundaries which may be set upon it and to permeate its surroundings. It thus stands in the sharpest possible opposition to individual formation and to self-containment: one need only consider the concepts of orgy, fornication, or things like tumorous growths, malarial parasites. Community in this sense should not however be confounded with a plenitude of relationships or with the relationship of love. It is not the reaching out and embracing, the experiencing of the nature of other beings which concerns us here, but rather the dissolution, the ceasing to exist, whether total or partial (the latter is more important for disgust) of alien beings. The manner in which the object of disgust accosts us and darts out towards us in snakelike fashion is not that of an unrequited or otherwise mistaken love; it involves much more elements of maliciousness, lovelessness, a striving for one's being, a sneering smirk at the affinity to this disgusting formation from which we find we cannot divert ourselves. Here it is not a question of unification, of our becoming firmly attached together, but of a fusion and confusion without restraint and of which the other side of the coin is decomposition, pulverization, universal indifference. In its full intention it is death and not life that announces itself to us in the phenomenon of disgust.

(b) What is most characteristic of the intention towards death in the instigation of disgust is that this thoroughly pervades also its own life-intention, as if through the surplus of life that is here so pronounced we were to become caught, as it were, in a short-circuit towards death, as if this intensified and concentrated life should have arisen out of an impatient longing for death, a desire to waste away, to over-spend the energy of life, a macabre debauchery of matter. For at first there always lies herein a life that is impoverished in its dimensions in spite of the moment of over-emphasized 'fullness'; there is to be found a desertion of the aggregate structure of life, an effervescent pursuing of one particular line of development. The intentional backgrounds, the contextual perspectives, the character of integratedness are here absent: life becomes condensed into an essentially homogeneous 'fluid'. (Compare also the life-character of putrefied or waste substances, of teeming vermin, of misplaced intellectual extravagance.) In this surplus of life itself there resides non-life, death. That passing into death through the cumulation of life has a character which is peculiarly distorted in comparison with simple dying or ceasing to exist. It is as if we acquire a fascination, as is often the case with disgusting objects, with a kind of vitality somehow conjured up within the framework of death. What is disgusting in a diluted, barely intimated form has a certain relation to the piquant. For there lies in the nature of the disgusting object, in its features [*Sosein*] rather than in its existential usefulness, something that is at first, as it were, an almost value-neutral invitation to concern oneself with it. But this alters nothing in its character of being always pregnant with death. In the most typical cases the disgusting object approaches in visible steps towards its own disintegration, whether in the form of decomposition to putridity, of disorganization, of dispersion, of being taken over by inferior, grosser, vital forces (for example in social life through dictatorship and the consequent sinking in a morass, after a period of corruption, in all its marshy flowering fullness). Particularly noteworthy is one type of potentially disgusting luxuriance of life which, although exhibiting poverty and homogeneity and linearity of development, does not include—ignoring certain metaphysical suppositions—pathological degeneration, namely extreme propagation and growth. There is here an intention of a rapidly encountered death, an over-accentuation of the rise and fall of life; one need only bring to mind the phenomenon of swarms of gnats or midges. To the individual, the formed unit of life here signifies nothing but death. Formations of this kind seem to lend justice to Schopenhauer's idea of life impulse, the thesis that the proper meaning of life is death. In all this shortness and abortiveness of life, co-ordinated with frenetic rapidity and furious zest for life there is something disgusting, as doubtless there is also (for the European) in the tropical rhythms of physiological and also vegetative life.

The intention towards death which now further presents itself is what relates to the individual's own lived existence [*Dasein*] and which turns upon the harmfulness of disgusting objects, their aggressiveness—the threat to transfer the decay and decomposition, effective within themselves, to everything with which they come in contact. This need not mean that the decomposition spreads itself in the same form as, for example, a contagious disease, but that in some way or other, on the basis of a kind of traffic with its victim, it creates disintegration and causes weakening, although not in a purely inimical way as straightforward poison, but still to some extent in an infectious manner. While it is not at all the case, however, that everything disgusting is also harmful, such a relation does certainly exist in important cases: the poisonousness of putrescent substances, the maliciousness of insects, the malevolent impulse of moral depravity to spread itself out. Clearly however in our image of disgusting objects as such, the moments of dangerousness and thus also of its significance in general for our own individual existence never holds a central position. Where this is the case, there exists fear and not disgust. In fact, disgusting formations are very often preponderate objects of fear, of horror, are very often terrifying or sinister. As long as it is disgust, however, that predominates, then it will be the intrinsic features of the object's *consistency*, including its effusiveness and aggressiveness, which will be intended, not the danger emanating from it. For if the latter is to take effect at all, it is in general presupposed that the subject should more or less voluntarily turn towards and approach the object: that, for example, he does in fact eat the spoiled food. Further the feared effect of the disgusting formation is rather intended only as a peripheral, molesting effect, not as something deadly which cuts into and permeates our life. One fears that one might become soiled by the object, or stuck to it, maybe even that one might enter into some form of lasting communion or somehow injurious relationship with it whereby our personality will become stained. We do not however fear that we might die or be gravely harmed physically (thus the fear is not one which rests on an intention towards our own total condition), nor that we might become so united metaphysically with the object that one might lose oneself in it. (Even the latter intention corresponds much more to anxiety or fear.) In disgust we do not at all think of the *consequences* of a closer, more active contact with the object but rather of the reinforcement of the moment of proximity, of the threatened intensification of the disgust itself which is brought about through our becoming further immersed in the object. Our attention at any rate is also drawn to the aggressive nature of the object; its desire to molest and the correlated tendency on our part to raise a defense, its character of being itself such as to dissuade the subject from affirming its proximity. Thus, the intention towards death mentioned above refers the disgusted person not to his dying or his state thereafter or to the passing away of his intellectual and moral self, but rather—insofar as his own person is co-intended at all, which is the case already on the strength of a possible proximity—to his being shifted into the sphere of death and of what is saturated by death, although with a reference back to his own affinity with it, but not as regards changing his fate. We arrive at this point at the question as to the nature of the challenge or provocation that is involved in disgust.

The challenge that emanates from what is disgusting has a double sense in conformity with the ambivalence of disgust described in Section II. It is at one and the same time both invitation and deterrent, both inducement and threat; the 'coquetry' which is inherent in disgust has already been recognized by decadent poetry. Certainly, it is the negative that prevails therein: the underlying positive element only increases through the vehemence of the defense reaction, since the latter still has to prevail against something which we feel simultaneously tempted to approach. Naturally, it is not in the least as though the attraction were inverted into repugnance simply by some mystical kind of pressure of culture and upbringing. The element of repulsion, likewise, is present as something firmly rooted therein. However it is as if it were only this invitation that actualizes the repugnance. We shun what is disgusting only because otherwise we should take hold of it, something which must not happen—originally not as a result of some disadvantageous experience of its consequences—but rather on the strength of a genuine reference to the features of the object [*Soseinsbezugnahme*].

Crudely speaking, the challenge which is to be found in disgust shows itself substantially in the fact that the object signifies to the subject at one and the same time both life and death (the latter in the irrevocable, overwhelming sense) and draws both tightly towards it. The provocation which is brought about by the surplus of life which here presents itself is explained by the connection to functional aspects of the subject-person: there arises for the latter the temptation to eat the object, to touch it, and so forth. But the intention towards death, too, is something that strikes the disgusted subject immediately; the stimulation and subsequent inner denial can be made responsible only for the actualization and redundancy of the defense, not for the formation of the attitude of defense itself. This contact rests on the affinity of the person's feeling with that deathly life. The latter does not threaten only as a dangerous object might threaten which is at the same time also beautiful and therefore experienced as doubly menacing (for example a beautiful tiger, a grandiose waterfall, which are anything but disgusting—as little as is, say, a beautiful yet domineering woman, or a tasty but prohibited dish). Rather, there exists here also a certain intimate, albeit disavowed relation to the essential feature of the matter [*Wesens-(Soseins-) beziehung*]. The ugly face of death which seems to present itself to us in every disgusting object reminds us of our own affinity to death, of our inevitable submission to it, of our secret death wish. Thus it warns us not, as with the skull and the hourglass, of our own

existential inability to escape from death—similar to the experience
of the merciless approach of the hour of his execution of one who
has been sentenced to death—but rather of the subjection to death
which is essential to us, of the directedness towards death of our life
itself, of our existence as made up of material which is consecrated
to death; one could also say that we are drowned within a material
which is already prepared for decay. The disgusting object does not
hold before our eyes an hourglass but a distorting-mirror; it shows
us not a skull in its dry eternity but rather precisely what no longer
attaches to the skull and is still a matter of fluid decay.

It is not, however, as though disgust would mean fear at or horror of one's own dissolution, nor a concern with one's own vulner-
ability. It is much more a state of nausea that is related to the object:
a rushing through its features, through its so-being, which culmi-
nates in a final pushing away directed against it. It is only when we
subsequently reflect and meditate on what is disgusting and on disgust itself and when we become aware of our own destiny as food
for worms, that we fall into the just-mentioned attitude of fear or
horror. It has a place in disgust itself only insofar as one is disgusted
by, say, parts of one's own body or of one's own life. But in the
foreground of the phenomenon of disgust there remains the object
with its specific features or, more precisely, with its features
together with the peculiarly accentuated moment of existential
proximity. Such a powerful instinctual reaction of 'pushing away'
would of course be impossible under conditions of complete
putting out of action of the moment of concern over one's own
existence (of the sort which occurs at the maximal limit in the attitude of aesthetic evaluation). But this intention towards existence is
not directed simply to one's own situation (one's own survival), as
this is subject to the causal efficacy of the object, but rather through
its proximity—proximity as sensual perceivability, as palpability, as
the closeness of functional relation, traffic, communion with the
object. We might call this a substantial proximity. Like every actual
proximity it may come about accidentally; but it exists in the fullest
sense only in virtue of the peculiar nature, the peculiar effort of the
subject involved. It is a 'metaphysical surrounding'. This is not the
only case where the existential situation becomes conditioned and
formed by a plenitude of features and where, on the other side, the
existential situation itself is again represented in featural determina-

tions and permeates the latter. For it is this which—as already intimated—first permits us in some way to grasp the matter: this substantial proximity which touches the *general* properties of our being
and at the same time represents in a concentrated manner the specific features of the object giving rise to disgust. Disgust does not
present the subject's own self: for this it has too little actual effect
on his whole being, its influence on his intrinsic existential formation is too small. In the subject's experience it is the specific situation in which he finds himself that is mainly intended. (For this
experience relates certainly to human existence as such, but not—
except in special cases—to the peculiar personal problems of the
subject in question nor to the organic development of the events in
which he is involved.) Here this special situation, the proximity of
the object with its quite characteristic intention towards life and
towards death, constitutes a unity between the object itself and its
announcing of life and death. In the object itself there is a perverse
proximity of elements, a prevailing proximity, which signifies at one
and the same time the oppressiveness of life and the denial of the
life-forming tension—a proximity which of its inmost nature is
geared towards expansion and towards an avalanche-like swelling
up. The merely accidental being-in-sight of an object that is somehow near in this sense presents itself to the subject already as a fully
determined, aggressive, hot, sticky proximity. The object is given to
the individual as *this thing there pervaded by proximity*. Hence the
defense reaction of repulsion against it along with the intention
towards its features which is central to it. Here we come closer to
an understanding of the connection between the formal and material sense of the phenomenon of disgust, of its relation to the features of the object and its striving towards a defense against death
and its rejection of subservience to that sort of wallowing in life that
is life-betraying. Also, in this way we obtain a closer understanding
of the peculiar phenomenon whereby an object that of its nature
would not be disgusting can under certain circumstances appear to
be so through proximity—as in the case of satiety in regard to the
associated pleasure, or of an abominated sexual approach in regard
to the associated taste or body. Although what we have here is primarily a disgust relating to a state of affairs (in any case a more subtle, moral disgust), it concentrates itself where possible on the
intuitive object, with its unified set of features, which forms the

principal carrier of such morally relevant states of affairs. (In regard
to many other feeling impulses an 'associative transference' of a similar kind does not occur with such vehemence; thus, for example fear
at a certain possible turn of events will not by any means convert
itself automatically into fear of those human beings who may have
some part in bringing it about).

Finally we remark that the very possibility of all these various
arguments themselves, our initial hypothesis concerning the unity of
the phenomenon of disgust and also, in a certain sense, of what is
disgusting, may be confirmed. The affinity of what is morally disgusting with what is physically disgusting is not merely a matter of
the reproduction of certain formal relationships, but is much more
a substantial equality of essence, something which is confirmed also
by innumerable transitional phenomena (the vital urge as such, sexual urges, consciousness of satiety). This conclusion should also contribute to our appreciation of the significance of disgust as an
important constituent of life.

IV. On the Ethics of Disgust

Denn greulich vor uns, wildverschlungen floß
Ein Strom von Aas, auf dem die Sonne tanzte.
. . .
Ich nannt' mich Liebe, und nun packt mich auch
Dies Würgen vor dem scheußlichsten Gesetze—
. . .
Mein Vater du, so du mein Vater bist,
Laß mich doch lieben dies verweste Wesen,
Laß mich im Aase dein Erbarmen lesen:
Ist das denn Liebe, wo noch Ekel ist?!
. . .
Er neigte wild sich nieder und vergrub
Die Hände ins verderbliche Geziefer:
Und ach, von Rosen ein Geruch, ein tiefer,
Von seiner Weiße sich erhub.

(F. Werfel, *Jesus und der Äser-Weg*)

[For there floated loathsomely before us
A stream of carrion upon which the sun was dancing.
. . .
I had called myself love and now I, too, am seized
With retching before the most hideous of laws—
. . .
My Father as Thou my Father art,
Let me yet love this moldered being,
Let me read Thy mercy in the carrion:
Or is it love where still disgust remains?!
. . .
He threw himself wildly down to the ground
And buried his hands in the corrupted vermin:
And ah, a fragrance of roses so deep
Rose upwards from its whiteness.]

(F. Werfel, *Jesus and the Carrion Way*)

IV.1 *The Ethical Function of Disgust*

In the preceding section we treated a number of examples of the role of disgust in moral rejection and in our recognition of the unethical. That it plays such a role is not refuted, but is indeed confirmed by the fact that the phenomena of disgust and ethical condemnation do not appear in parallel with each other but only as linked together in a rather equivocal way. This holds still more for example in the case of hate and of similar feelings of disapproval. There belongs to the character of disgust its being bound up with a specific content, an 'irrational residue'. It stands, one might say, in irregular service of the morally good. Disgust is not a primary experience of evil; insofar as it relates to intellectual and ethical matters at all, it only points toward evil. More precisely, it indicates the presence of a particular quality of the unethical, namely, the morally 'putrid' or 'putrescent'. In order more closely to delineate this quality, we shall compare disgust with a related but more general feeling of moral reprobation: the feeling of *contempt*.

Although it does not accompany every act of denial of value to the same degree, contempt is pronouncedly a judgment-feeling [*Urteilsgefühl*]; it presupposes an unfavorable judgment about its object, not merely logically but in the actually experienced sense. Contempt is a possible reaction only to someone who is capable of and in the habit of making judgments. It is a type of position-taking which not only admits justification, but also bears its self-justification as it were on its face and which, in the event that it encounters real refutation, will as a matter of course become extinguished. On the other hand however, contempt also seems to contain in its straightforward feeling-character something that goes beyond the disapproving judgment: a shade of the biological, a tinge of disgust itself. In an individual case an object may give rise to a feeling of contempt wholly without any trace of disgust, but it seems to us that in general contempt presupposes the moment or tonality of disgust. In very many cases disgust and contempt are united in a single feeling of moral disapproval; one may indeed be contemptuous of someone 'as a worm'. Not everything that encounters ethical reprobation is at the same time an object of contempt and, even in experiences of value outside the ethical sphere, there is something that may rightly be referred to as contempt. Contempt is directed not simply towards what partakes of disvalue, but much more towards the mean, the unrefined, the inadequate, the unreliable—and indeed precisely wherever the object raises a pretension of value and seeks by force to curry favor from the subject. Here too is revealed the analogy with disgust, as though there were planted in the feeling of contempt a moment of formalized, cooled, and regulated disgust. Contempt and disgust are, then, consonant in that both are concerned with what is contrary to value and at the same time wretched, in a state of ruin, even if not in every respect but from certain essential points of view. Yet, contempt relates thereby more to the element of inadequacy, of ethical, willful inability to stand the test, of an inferior, wretched, animalistic apprehension of life. Disgust on the other hand relates more to the element of an unclean constitution correlated with a substantial putrefaction. Thus pettiness, though it may often be rather contemptible, is never disgusting; an over-fastidious and intellectualized lust will be much more disgusting than contemptible. An action can be contemptible, but it is in itself too abstract an entity to be an object of disgust. The latter will never direct itself against a naked deed as such, but rather perhaps against the personality of the agent that is expressed plastically in the action or against the concretely visible processes that are contained within the action or inextricably connected with it. On the other hand the sphere of disgust extends so far as to include such things as situations, conditions, material (which may thought to be unappetizing, unclean) which could in no way be worthy of contempt.

For this reason we ascribe to disgust an irreplaceable and legitimate ethical-cognitive function that cannot be exercised by contempt alone. To those, of course, who stand firmly by, say, the theory of the categorical imperative, such a view would be unacceptable. For an ethic of that kind knows only maxims of action and possibly also the character which may be derived therefrom. However a value-ethic which embraces all the tonalities and adumbrations of the moral sphere will not fail to recognize the efficacy of disgust in this field. It is certainly true that disgust does not attain normative certainty, as does contempt. Rather, it manifests an intimate intermingling with extra-ethical emotions of taste. In general it can only serve as a signpost towards a subsequent ethical judgement, and cannot be its immediate determining factor. In place of this, though, it is characterized by a spontaneity and originality, an intimacy of feeling, of sensing or perceiving, that is entirely absent from contempt, and thus is invaluable for the consolidation of an ethical orientation in concrete affairs.

What, however, is that type of evil, or better that kind of relation of a person towards evil, which is specifically suited to arouse disgust, and then in the judgement sphere to the evocation of the assertion that a person is 'unclean', is somehow tainted? Let us suppose that someone is wholly in the service of some bad cause or passion, or, at least to the extent that he is evil, he is fully consciously so, and declares what is ordinarily taken as evil to be the most authentic, valuable and incontestable good. (The structure of his intentions may exhibit here a large degree of variation.) This Satanism of the hardened criminal, even though it may extend to spheres of instinct and vital drives that are outside the power of will in the narrower sense, is neither contemptible in the primary sense of the term, nor disgusting. To perceive the criminal in this way, a metaphysical perspective would be required in which in the end the devil himself would have to figure as having been betrayed.

Phenomenologically speaking, however, neither contempt nor disgust would be an appropriate immediate response in this case. If someone who in his convictions is wholly committed to the good yet has elements of evil in himself, passions and weaknesses to which he succumbs here and there, or even in some sense continually, then this may be contemptible like any other weakness in moral life, but not properly disgusting, for this person cannot be said actually to live in evil. Another type of contemptibility is what relates to petty or trivial baseness, to what allows no doubt or inner struggle of any kind, but where the subject has already from the start concluded some kind of compromise with evil designed to help him more easily overcome the obstacles of life: thus, an attitude of life which is without ethical pretensions. This too does not belong to the proper domain of disgust: the phenomenon in question is too self-enclosed, too stable, too colorless, and also, we might say, somehow too healthy to be truly disgusting; that kind of immorality which above all others gives rise to disgust shows a quite different structure. It is exhibited by those characters who (1) manage to keep a certain distance between themselves and what is evil, are not firmly allied with evil, and do not simply dissociate themselves from ethical categories; (2) are not in a (possibly hopeless) conflict with evil, but are much more in a continually renewed, continually re-actualized embrace with it; allow themselves repeatedly to be conquered by it; and who therefore (3) experience evil, and are to the extent that this is presupposed thereby also engaged in an inner struggle with it that is however merely *pro forma*, they make a song and dance out of the circumstances of their moral life, get a kick out of it. It is here as if we were offered almost visually the process by which the substance of a person may become transformed into a state of putrefaction—in contrast to those truly Satanic types of hyperactivity, characteristic of the person striving, in a uniform fashion, towards evil (even, perhaps, towards their own metaphysical self-annihilation), and in contrast also to those states in which the subject is still somehow merely superficially conquered by what is evil and by those states which merely involve a comfortable paying of tribute to evil.

In moral putrefaction it is the innermost core of the person—that which relates most closely to his experiences, that which is, as it were, the most valuable in him—which is involved and which glows with a moldy phosphorescent sheen. It is not as if there rules an unequivocal and self-contained striving towards evil; rather what is originally at least potentially good and noble has here inclined over into depravity, into an attitude of irresponsible lustful excess. A certain dubitability, a repeatedly deceiving ambiguity of moral normativities is characteristic of this type of putrefaction, of moral *haut-goût*. Just as one is not at first sensible to the doubtful or suspect character of a dish one has been served which is no longer fresh—here the tonality of this 'no longer' is just as important. The human type we are dealing with here finds himself as if by destiny putrefied in a permanent motion towards what is evil. Persons of this kind also pretend sometimes to be not merely under constraint but subject to a fate that is 'beyond' morality and yet valuable. With the properly criminal type any comparison with putrefaction is less possible, since here there can be no question at all of a *de facto* process of decay of the person of the sort which takes place in the putrefaction of organic material.

Mental illness is also to this extent dissimilar to putrefaction: it contains no surplus of life and no death-intention within the framework of a given functional structure of life, but is rather a distortion of this structure itself. For this state does not at all affect life and death as substantial processes, but rather the empirical conditions of the total mental life of the subject. This is not to say that there cannot be also certain formations of mental illness which have effects similar to those of physical deformation in giving rise to disgust. In the central sense however only moral putrefaction is disgusting in bringing to light the as it were perverse, hysterical, underlying surrender of the value-elements of the soul to evil, personality-destroying forces and experiences. Here it is the content of the soul itself which becomes suspect and not free of the possibility of reproach; the content in its total significance becomes mendacious, it becomes itself and with all its values foul, pregnant with the process of putrefaction. That this type of human being can have something alluring or attractive about him is associated with his relation to disgust. But there is in fact here a greater possibility of deceit than is the case with the physically disgusting in consequence of its being less immediate and of less unambiguous urgency; as in cases of moral, as compared to physical reactions, even a truly criminal character is capable of deceiving a great deal more than is a wild animal or an immediately obviously dangerous human being.

Connected with the abuse of positive spiritual values and with the accentuated features [*Sosein*] of objects of disgust is the fact that the morally putrefied and the disgusting stand in a quite peculiarly close relation with the sphere of eroticism and further also to the habits of speech of the persons in question. We must however abstain here from any further description and classification of these phenomena of moral evil.

A word should however be added on the ethical importance of physical disgust. It is an accepted view that bodily cleanliness and orderliness, as well as the functioning of certain feelings of disgust which are standard in a given society, are of ethical relevance. This view does not rest merely on the hygienic significance of cleanliness, which is indeed somewhat exaggerated in the present day. If it is asserted that the externally grimy person is usually also grimy on the inside too, then it must also be pointed out that another type of human being has to be mentioned in whom there is combined over-scrupulous physical neatness with immorality. In every degree of cleanliness and susceptibility to disgust there may be implied a qualitatively different intention: negligence as such is not yet insensibility, and cleanliness can ensue either from genuine need for purity or out of an erotic tendency towards refinement, or even out of a desire to handle soiled material. In any case, a genuine absence of ability to experience physical disgust may signify also that the sense for what is ethically repugnant has atrophied, or may betray an inadequate development of feelings for demarcation and distance.

IV.2. *The Problem of Overcoming Disgust*

The idea which is presented by the extract from Werfel's beautiful poem serves our theme as a motto: the idea that disgust as well as anxiety can be overcome, and that this overcoming is ethically meritorious has been put forward already in a number of different variations. We shall try to elucidate some aspects of this problem without going into the parallels with bravery and cowardice: one's own existence [*Dasein*], danger, our experience of communication, physical contact with alien so-being [*Sosein*]—these are from the ethical point of view the most different things imaginable.

There are in the first place two fundamental distinctions to be made. From the practical and functional point of view there exist two kinds of disgusting objects: those which are, as it were, disgusting by their very nature and those which become so only under certain special circumstances. To the first group belong in particular excrements and putrescent matter in general: the waste products of nature, eliminated and expelled from the mechanism of life. The invitation that proceeds from them is unequivocally overwhelmed by the effects of their repulsive character. The disgust-sensation directed against such objects is something natural, something in the strictest sense adequate or appropriate to its object; 'disgusting' is here an autonomous characterization as much as a designation of color or of consistency would be. The matter is different in relation to objects which still somehow retain their capacity to function, are still somehow holding on to life: food, animals, living formations generally. Here the feeling of disgust—however generalized it may be—is always more a matter of will, depends more on a decision of the subject in the cause of its own resistance. In situations of this kind revision of the attitude towards disgust is, as a matter of principle, more appropriate.

The second differentiation relates to the 'pretension' which is in some cases exhibited by or resides in the abhorrent object. While certain disgusting formations are entirely passive in relation to the perceiving subject, as long as we do not seek them out they do not exist for us (for example many kinds of insect). But often such formations present an ostentatious aggressive actual proximity, which may have a lasting character and as it were force itself upon us (for example dirt). What we have here is indeed more than proximity, it is a relation which has about it a compulsive element, a pretension to value on the part of the object, an attempt on its part to establish itself firmly in our life. This is the case when a person's advances are experienced as disgusting or when a person presses him- or herself into the limelight, expressing a mentality that we find disgusting. The judgment of disgust itself is here to be conceived as follows: on the one hand there is in this second case (that is, of the pretentious object) more the danger of a rash and short-sighted retreat into the attitude of disgust and of the overlooking of values that are present. On the other hand, however, the justification for the subject's actually becoming disgusted may be greater, and it can much less be regarded as merely a matter of a capricious, as it were, 'reveling' in a state of disgust-addiction.

On the basis of the foregoing it will now be easy to understand the decisive distinction. This relates to the *kind* of rejection-intention inherent in the phenomenon of disgust. In fact the suppression of disgust can be required of or at least suggested to the subject in a twofold sense. In the sense that a feeling of disgust should not be allowed to justify the intention simply to destroy the relevant object, disgust ought not to signify: 'this object is to be destroyed'. Disgust alone cannot exhaustively determine our attitude towards an object, least of all where it is bound up with feelings of resentment and this especially in the case of 'disgusting human beings'—in contrast to the case of objects that are unequivocally disgusting but also necessities of nature (waste products). Disgust must not be allowed to blot out our love for a person or more generally for those things which represent culture. Besides the mere reactions of defense, of rejection, or of struggle, there must also always be taken into consideration at least the possibility of a change of heart or even of an affirmation for the sake of the valuable partial elements inherent in a person. Thus, a conquering of disgust in the sense of a state or condition is then in principle capable of being demanded, so that in cases of practical necessity the proximity of disgusting objects or the courageous handling of them become bearable by habit and by a certain technique and by a deadening of some reactions. As in the former case, where it was a question of the intentional restriction and relativization, so here we are dealing with an actual mental overcoming of disgust, naturally including also the cases where this is a matter of routine. There are also fields where both of these demands are interconnected; for example in charitable service, as contrasted with scientific research, where on the one side feelings of disgust have to be overcome purely because they interfere with the work in hand, but at the same time and in a more profound sense they will be overcome here because of a profounder attitude of love towards humanity.

But we are decidedly against the overcoming of disgust if this ideal is to take the form of a conception of disgust as a kind of narrow-minded prejudice, a product of morbid imagination, an insult to nature, or anything like that, and therefore something that has to be resisted by every means. (I once read the aphorism: 'Nothing is disgusting except disgust itself'!) Also, we are in no sense in agreement with the demand for a universal deadening or blunting of disgust to the level where we are unable to feel it at all. To take a position of this kind is rooted partly in that most pitiable type of epistemological subjectivism which dares not acknowledge the multi-layered richness of tensions of the world except as a product of imagination, and which recoils in horror even at the suggestion that there exist objective value and disvalue characters because this is taken as being 'unscientific'. But it is rooted partly also in that kind of naturalistic, pseudo-optimistic and immoralistic stupidity which begins to whine in protest at any more powerful accentuation of the negative: that this is a crime against nature, a matter, say, of bare prejudice, or monkish fanaticism. In opposition to this we would wish once again to emphasize the undeniable cognitive and selective task of disgust from the standpoint of biology, metaphysics, and ethics. To want to transcend or overcome disgust in light of these fundamental justifications of its significance is both a violent form of naturalism, alien to modesty and chastity, and—in relation to the subject of disgust—an equally violent Manichaeism, which despises reality and is 'idealistic' in the worst sense. It is not this kind of mechanistic distinction-blurring point of view but much rather the Christian concept of the summit of ethical perfection which is represented in the poem *Jesus and the Carrion Way*, which so perfectly embodies the spirit of the gospel. The disgusting object appears therein as thoroughly real; the Savior Himself (like His apostles) is choked with disgust at the sight of the carrion-stream. But He, the prophet of a love which knows no absolute bounds (though a multiplicity of gradations), beseeches God that that love may descend which is more powerful than disgust. Love that is *stronger* than disgust, but does not stand in place of a disgust that is merely a product of imagination, nor as in some way perversely connected therewith. Having partaken in this love, He plunges His hands into the seething mass of carrion; and He, the Savior, the apex of the divine in man, works a miracle. With a firm hand the poet selects the miracle of a fragrance of roses, announcing the victory of love over disgust, the non-finality, the merely relative dominion of decay. It is not however that the odor of carrion itself is suddenly experienced as agreeable, and it is in no way as if the given abhorrent formation is changed into something attractive in order to give the lie to disgust:

Er aber füllte seine Haare aus
Mit kleinem Aas und kränzte sich mit Schleichen
. . .
Und wie er so im dunkeln Tage stand,
Brachen die Berge auf und Löwen weinten
An seinem Knie . . .

[But he filled his hair
With little carrion and garlanded himself with worms—
. . .
And standing thus on that dark day
The mountains did break open and the lions wept
At his knee . . .]

It would be wrong to regard the human phenomenon to which
we have dedicated these reflections as any kind of aberration; rather
we should see it as something meaningful and legitimate in itself,
which when yielded to in an uncontrolled way may also bar us from
many of the values of life and hinder us in the performance of many
noble deeds, and which should, accordingly, be subjected to
repeated scrutiny, to repeated honing and illumination.

Concluding Bibliographical Remark

Our subject does not lend itself well to the pernicious practice of
bibliographical meticulousness. The little which can be found scattered on our subject in the literature is not very informative. W.
Wundt (*Physiologische Psychologie*, 5th ed., Leipzig, 1902, pp. 54f)
can talk in regard to disgust only of "bitter and salty taste-impres-
sions." This is more or less as if one were to exhaust the problem of
religious experience with a reference to "the majesty of mountains."
O. Külpe all too laconically also spares himself the trouble of a closer
investigation: "Disgust, formerly classified as a sensation of taste, is
probably an aversion which makes its appearance in connection with
muscle sensations preceding vomiting" (*Grundzüge der Psychologie*,
Leipzig, 1893, p. 102). Dread [*das Grausen*], as a synthesis of disgust and fright, is mentioned by J. Volkelt (*System der Ästhetik*, 2nd
ed., Munich, 1925, p. 160). Important motives of disgust are how-

ever pointed out by the Hegelian K. Rosenkranz (*Ästhetik des Hässlichen*), Königsberg, 1853, pp. 312ff), who mentions: dissolution of what is already dead—"secretion"—inorganic nature as disgusting only by analogy—the highest made most lowly—and so forth.

The Standard Modes of Aversion: Fear, Disgust, and Hatred

AUREL KOLNAI

1. Introduction

I have nothing to offer but (a) one very plain and unexciting thesis of *asymmetry* between the fundamental types of emotional responses (or responses and reactions) to objects: liking and disliking, or, say, pro and con, appreciative/appetitive and aversive: an asymmetry not just empirically encountered but analyzable and explainable; and (b) a restricted and somewhat arbitrary triadic selection of modes of aversion on which to base a differential analysis. I shall argue that no such fundamental division, that is, none exactly on the same logical footing with this, can be attempted in the vastly more variegated range of friendly responses; and shall also mildly try to uphold the fairly representative character of the chosen triad of fear, disgust, hatred.

Certainly we are accustomed to such apparently symmetrical contrasts as like and dislike, pro and con, being pleased and displeased, appetite and repugnance, attraction and aversion, love and hatred. That appearance of symmetry is near enough to evident truth so long as we stick closely to the highly general root concepts of pro and con, like and dislike, or acceptance and rejection. It tends, however, to break down as our interest turns to the specified forms of pro and con emotional attitudes. Is hatred a symmetrical opposite of love? In every language, the word 'love' has a way of embracing the entire conceptual field of pro responses: hence the traditional trinity of *amor complacentiae*, *amor concupiscentiae*, and *amor benevolentiae*. Hatred is confined within much narrower limits: its proper object is only a person or a collective of persons, or at any rate something strictly expressive of the attitudes or words of such. In other cases, loathing, detestation, or repugnance rather than hatred seems to be the fit counterpart of what may still quite properly be called love. I love the ducks in the park; I would refuse to say that I 'hate' the seagulls which infest it in wintertime. Again, disgust has its range of objects limited to live beings or their remains, products, vestiges or representations; there is no similarly classic counterpart to it on the pro side. Again, what is the opposite of fear? Perhaps trust or gratitude? Or feeling of safety or coziness or of tranquility? Deriving encouragement from? But these are very heterogeneous among themselves; only trust (or gratitude) is necessarily directed to an intentional object, and it has much more specific meaning than a mere negation of fear. What is common to this bunch of 'opposites' is precisely only the absence of fear and nothing as definite and sharply profiled as fear.

2. The Concept of Emotive Responses

The present survey concerns (a few outstanding) 'emotive responses', something closely germane I think to Meinong's *emotionale Präsentation*, meaning thereby acts or attitudes or conative states of consciousness which on the one hand are clearly governed by an intentional object, and on the other hand express something like a passion aroused in the self, an impact exercised upon it down to its somatic sounding-board; in other words intention (*Gegenständlichkeit*) as linked essentially, though not in a uniform or unequivocal or causally necessary fashion, to condition (*Zuständlichkeit*). This close linkage is emphasized in both phrasings: 'emotive response' and, more profoundly perhaps, 'emotional presentation'. I shall try to show that the linkage is multiform not only in the obvious content-related sense (a shuddering or an aggressive, etc., response to different objects which is built into their modes of presentation), but also in a structural sense (condition adhering to intention in different manners in fear and disgust, etc.). Our range of interest here is marked off, on the one side, against a more or less purely judgment-like and, in spite of the pro or con sign, intellectual apprehension; and, on the other side, against such almost pure condition-types as joy, depression or excitement, causally induced in whatever way and possibly, but non-obligatorily and perhaps quite vaguely, tied to intentional awareness (that is, to the presentation of an object). In other words still, our interest fastens on the intimate and as it were indissoluble juncture-point between objects as intentionally present and the possible correlative motions of the soul as somehow significantly involving states of the body. Should anyone ask what justifies the constitution of a philosophic interest of this kind, I ask leave to demur. I would just briefly and opaquely hint that inquiries of such a kind might contribute to the elucidation of the mystery of practice, or call it the logic of practice, including the highly elusive problem—be it a problem not only elusive but delusive, or as I feel meaningful and central—of adequate and inadequate emotive attitudes.

3. Some Self-Objections

I readily admit the probable existence of far more felicitous models than mine (fear, disgust, hatred). My modest claim is only that one selective analysis of aversions thus arranged might easily be worth more than none. Anyhow, it will not unreasonably be asked why I have left out contempt, indignation, horror, awe, *Grauen* (stupefying, deep-toned horror, dear to Germans), *Grausen* (horror with overtone of fear and a dominant of disgust), *Gruseln* (cosy shivering with tempered fear),[1] irritation, boredom, anxiety, and anguish as distinct from fear and from each other, and above all of course anger, not to forget loathing and detestation. I might turn to some of these another time, or, much better, hope that they might tempt more competent analysts. But I would at least suggest that for the present purpose some of these modes are both too episodic and one-sidedly emotional (anger: too pictorial as it were; and incapable of a sustained form distinct from hatred); or on the contrary not emotional enough and too near to mere depreciation and dislike (contempt and detestation); or too imprecise to grasp, or too narrowly specific or too obviously synthetic. (As to anger: does it not connote a mood of eager, lusty, serene, and enterprising aggressiveness, perhaps entirely devoid of hostility?) Granted: disgust may be attacked on the ground of its somewhat restricted range; I have to gently stretch the concept without lapsing into a trivial misuse of language, and in a way which has some point. Again, hatred may seem too vast and complex a phenomenon, and collapse into anger if we look for its *actuel* (episodic, condition-like) aspect; still, I feel I must not resist the appeal of its classic dignity nor my confident belief as a moralist in its unequivocal hard core. Anguish: if it means more than intense fear, is it not mainly a matter for medical science? The trouble with anxiety is that I doubt the existence of 'free-floating anxiety', and suspect the concept of being a product of intellectual sloth and mystagogic irrationalism. I am so overwhelmed with fears of this or that and most things that I can't muster time or interest to be afraid of nothing in particular into the bargain. There are of course vague fears of things which seem to threaten us and which we are unfamiliar with and know but dimly. (There is also the anxious disposition easily actualized: the worrying temper.)

Some other hostile attitudes, such as envy, resentment, and rivalry, may be just mentioned in passing. They are distinguished by the conspicuous thematic status, in their make-up, of specified *good* (that is, objects of pro-attitudes) which the agent experiences as lost, in danger of being lost, near-lost, or near-missed which he equates to lost.

And something basic and perhaps most important has been left so far in complete obscurity. Of what ontological types are the intentional objects we have here in mind? How far are they concrete entities, 'individuals'; how far, features; how far, events? This is part of a larger question altogether beyond our present scope. Do we desire a thing, or (only) our functional use or enjoyment of it? Appreciation has a different grammar from desire; wanting, on the contrary, seems to be more definitely situation-directed than desiring. How do the purely feature-orientated, analytical components of love relate to its thisness-orientated aspects, its historical and uniqueness-emphasizing aspects? It would at any rate appear to me as if the reference to features, to qualities displayed, were most conspicuously present in disgust; the reference to individual entity, in hatred; and, above all, the reference to situation and causal mechanism of events, in fear. Let me now try to sketch the respective structures of these three modes of aversion.

4. Fear and Flight (*fuga*)

The agent in fear flees the object which he feels threatens his survival, safety, welfare, or any of his vital interests—the integrity of his possessions, body, or status in any sense (including chances or prospects). 'Flight', in its simplest and most elemental form, 'running away', means the action—the motion—of setting himself at a distance from the radius of operation of the threatening object; his shutting himself off, completely and definitively or so far as possible, against its power of attack; his putting himself beyond its reach. The description needs manifold qualifications, but remains, I think, substantially correct; it designates at any rate the focal meaning of what is the case. It applies to the bare state of fear as such, even if for the time being nothing actually happens in the sense of physical movement or of conceiving a specific design of self-protection. The structure of fear is not altered by the agent's concern involving another person or several such (to whom he is in some way linked), or even by its being centered on persons or animals other than himself. Flight need not literally mean running away, traveling to a distant place, or going into hiding. It is not the spatial proximity of the feared object but the agent's being actually or virtually exposed to its impact that matters. The person actuated by fear may aim at parrying the blow of his pursuer, setting up a protective barrier, preventively destroying the threatening agent or conjunction of forces, neutralizing its hurting power (for example, by undergoing immunization or destroying potential weapons of an enemy, etc.). Flight, then, may take the form of averting an impending danger rather than fleeing a presence; fear means eminently aversion in a more literal sense of the term than 'antipathy'. Its point lies in the agent's endeavor to extricate himself from, or guard against his becoming involved in, a causal nexus in the machinery of which he sees himself (or persons or goods he sets store by, in whose fate he is involved) as the victim or sufferer. (The fate of what I am concerned for is part of my fate.)

Fear is obviously most sharply condition-orientated: he who is frightened or afraid has his safety and his danger in mind—greatly more so than he who feels disgust, anger, or hatred. Often and typically he fears, directly or at least by implication, for his life. But in one sense, and I shall presently return to this, the condition-

emphasis of fear falls short of that of disgust and anger, if not perhaps of hatred. Let me first advert to the intentionality inherent in
fear.

Aside from the problematic phenomenon of objectless or 'free-
floating' anxiety, fear is no doubt keenly aware of its object. That
fear may be imaginary or repose on a well-defined error does not
detract at all from this awareness. The real object need not coin-
cide with the intentional object; it may be simply non-existent (for
example, fear of ghosts in a haunted castle at night is in no wise
objectless anxiety, though most likely no ghosts are on the
premises at all, and even though the timorous believer in ghosts
may have only a very vague notion of what they are like and of the
harm he is liable to suffer at their hands). However, the intentionality of fear is neatly circumscribed by the fact that fear as such is
not intrinsically interested in its object. It is different if fear is associated with fascination or loathing or hatred, which is often the
case (for example, fear of tigers, women, smallpox)—though it
need not be the case at all. (I fear air travel, don't particularly
loathe it and much less desire it, and know next to nothing about
it.) What interests us about the fearsome, terrible, or dangerous
object as such is only the threat it embodies, and thus not properly
speaking its nature or value and disvalue, not the landscape of its
features and qualities. There is some analogy between fear and an
instrumental pro-attitude such as our wish for an object that we
intend to apply to a given purpose, without being interested in it
'for its own sake'. It may thus be said that fear carries in it a purely
circumstantial, unidimensional, as it were skeleton-like and
'unfilled' intentionality. No doubt it may stimulate—indeed,
necessitate or compel—a keen study, perhaps a minute descriptive
knowledge, of its object: but that remains wholly subordinate to
the dominant theme of averting its threat to our own security (in
whatever respect).

Hence, the 'quality' of fearfulness, terribleness or (and what I
mean comes out best in *this* word) dangerousness of the feared
object has a dubious status, lending support to a relativistic
approach. A cat, even a robust kitten, appears 'terrible' to a mouse
or a small bird but to me it is only lovely, fascinating, and adorable.
(Yet I may be displeased by its wanton and frivolous cruelty: a true
objective property.) The caged beasts of prey in a zoo may appear

fearsome but still fail to inspire actual fear in their onlookers, in spite of the beasts' nearness and their presumed or even manifest sanguinary impulses; the quality of fearsomeness is cancelled or annulled, or say bracketed, by the circumstance that they cannot *de facto* get at the public and hurt or chase it. The almost invariable and complete absence of fear in the visitors reveals the distinctive subjection of that mode of aversion to rational control—as contrasted with disgust, loathing and 'essential' dislike (and *pro tanto* hatred), and as contrasted with emotive attitudes dependent on 'taste'. Fear is highly susceptible of being unfastened from its object by convincing argument and cognitive discovery. (But I admit that to some extent this thesis is contradicted by certain particular and obsessive fears occurring in a number of people. Mice? Ghosts? I fear the browse.)[2]

Notwithstanding its frequently observable heavy somatic resonance (fright, trembling, pallor, palpitation), I would suggest that fear somehow lacks body, as it were, on the condition side. Owing to its concentration on *Dasein*, on the survival interest with its toned-down corollaries such as unruffled comfort and security, fear is apt to restrict the self-experience of the person to an abstract and jejune experience of 'being affected' and imperiled qua 'existent self'. The reductionist metaphysical embroideries of Heidegger (man is just *Dasein*, *Angst*, and *Sorge*), Franklin Roosevelt (the utopia of freedom from fear), and Hobbes, by far the most sensible of the three (men's most urgent business: to create some foolproof safety against extermination), may be mentioned in passing. The essential poverty of fear-intentionality is mirrored in the constricted linearity of the fear condition. It is as a disgusted self that I inscribe my quality and lineaments into the stuff of the world, and as a hating self that I set the seal of my personality on a universe reluctant but vulnerable like myself. And even if I assert myself much less, I unfold vastly more in love.

5. Disgust and Ejection (or Avulsion, or Specific Aversion)

Disgust, in contrast with fear, bears exquisitely on *Sosein*—the sensible and perceptible nature of things, as distinct from their causal efficiency and impact. So far, the intention of disgust adheres to and penetrates its objects rather than merely signaling and portending their disquieting presence or proximity; it is inseparable from an intrinsic interest in the object. Spatial or at any rate imaged and representational nearness is thematic to disgust as it is not to fear. In disgust too we perform a sort of 'flight'; it is not flight from the object's radius of action, however, but from its perceptual neighborhood and from possible contact, and most of all a possible intimate contact and union with it. As a movement of flight and turning-away, disgust, in contradistinction from hatred, still resembles the passivity of fear; but in its aspect of essential rejection and analytical (hostile) interest in the object 'for its own sake', it resembles hatred as opposed to fear. Again, in virtue of its perceptual emphasis, disgust is set in contrast with fear and hatred alike. It lacks, comparatively speaking, the existential note of fear and hatred; the person seized with disgust does not 'run for his life', nor does he in any direct and emphatic sense seek to destroy (diminish, weaken, humiliate, reduce, etc.) the object of his aversion. He is merely intent on eliminating it from his ken and avoiding its contact. This may of course practically, not to say technically, issue in a will to destroy it; but so may fear. And, in a secondary sense, we also fear what disgusts us, and may actually run away from it; yet there is likewise some interconnection between fear and hatred (I fear the reaction against myself and the influence on others of what I hate, etc.).

In keeping with its non-existential and perceptual emphasis, disgust is an eminently *aesthetic* emotion, though undoubtedly an object may be very ugly without being disgusting, and may even be disgusting while being only moderately and perhaps only ambiguously ugly (for example, some disgusting insects, or a dressed-up harlot). And 'disgusting' is a more properly and descriptively object-characterizing word than 'fearsome' or 'terrible' on the one hand, 'odious' or 'hateful' (*haïssable, hassenswert*) on the other. The disgusting is exquisitely what provokes disgust as a proper response, whereas an object is 'fearful' or 'redoubtable' (*terrible*) in virtue of the actual or virtual (anticipated) fear it inspires in us, and—notwithstanding the presupposed primary disvalue of what we hate—our hatred goes to constitute the 'odiousness' of its intentional object. 'The disgusting' then is susceptible of a *self-contained* phenomenological description far more than either 'the fearsome' or 'the odious'.

All the same, even apart from the factor of circumstantial nearness, disgust is not wholly independent of the situational presentation of the object. Thus, while a man will not feel a male body to be disgusting, he might experience a male body amorously pressing against his as disgusting, without experiencing a female body in that way, however indecently obtruding. The reference of disgust to an incipient or possible intimate contact (union, communion, relation of absorption or assimilation) with its object underlies three obvious and familiar aspects of it.

(1) Ambivalence, that is, an innuendo, somehow or other present in the disgust-intention and expressed in the object, of attraction, temptation, *Reiz* (charm, spell, fascination as it were); a tinge of the taunting; the repulsiveness of what might solicit acceptance and enjoyment. While the synthetic word 'disgust' (*dégoût*) has a less forceful and specific ring than the original and unitary or all-of-a-piece terms, *Ekel* and *asco*, signifying in their own right, still it is more expressive, in as much as it carries within it the echo of a negated 'gusto'. ('I am disgusted', *être dégoûté de quelque chose*: these point to displeasure, in the place of disgust proper. They substitute the irksome for the nauseating. In Spanish, *disgusto* never means disgust, but displeasure, calamity, or setback.)

(2) The gustatory and olfactory sphere appears to be the primary habitat of disgust. A frightful reek 'stinks in our nostrils', it has invaded us and intruded into our corporeal intimacy. (Smelling, on our part, is *par excellence* probing.) In nausea and vomiting, we *eject* what has in a more massive sense infested our body, possibly with our own initial consent. Yet any rigid interpretation of disgust in terms of vomiting or retching, or the tendency to it, is open to the charge of a mistaken simplification. Many kinds of vomiting are associated either with a feeling of nausea but scarcely with any disgust-intention, or with vertigo rather than nausea; they may be due to wholly non-alimentary somatic causes. Moreover, an attempt to chew and swallow non-comestible stuff (say wood or sawdust) is likely to conjure up vomiting without any feeling of disgust proper; and, while some kinds of food or drink we violently dislike strike us as disgusting, others do not.[3] Again, visual disgust quite outside the sphere of taste and smell may be

extremely powerful. Thus, insects crawling and squirming—perhaps our disgust is aware of the possibility of their creeping upon our body and, worse, their entering our mouth? Certainly the aspect of being in motion materially contributes to the disgustingness of objects of this kind.[4] (A question: does auditory disgust exist? The sense object of hearing—sound—is said to be *in* the ear; on the other hand, sound merely 'signals' rather than exhibits the ontological object, the "thing" which emits or produces it [hearing being a 'causal' mode of sensing]. Perhaps a 'fat' chuckle and some forms of music [jazz, some Viennese waltz] sound disgusting; but we are leaving here the realm of primary, physical, and approaching that of moral disgust.)

(3) Putrescence, excreta and secreta, dissolution and decomposition of organic matter form a classic area of predilection for disgust. Close relations, which I have no space to go into now, subsist with the sting of danger and a potentiality of fear but also with a feature of macabre attractiveness; with the idea of adhesive contact; with the experience of so-called 'vermin'; and also with the phenomenon of so-called 'dirt': the limiting case of an unfitting adherence to the body of partly at least inorganic amorphous matter as an object of disgust. Now what disgust refers to here is certainly not lifelessness as such, or even dying and death: a skeleton, a mummy, the sight of a moribund person are perhaps depressing but not disgusting; whereas wounds, and even more skin rashes, may well be. The deformation and detritus of life are certainly candidate themes; but what must be added is its inordinate, unruly, crowded, teeming and pullulating, heaving and as it were unmeaning manifestation as well. Incipient putrescence is apt to throw the aroma of a substance (for a while) into higher relief: we actually speak of venison that is 'high', of *haut goût*. (Cf. the odor of a scented person, calculated to exert attraction, and often felt as disgusting; it is alleged that excrement is used in the manufacture of some scents.) Again the phenomenon of surfeit and the quality of the 'cloying' have their place in this context. It might be argued that the emphatic, obtrusive, and excessive manifestation of life as such tends to arouse disgust; and similarly, the absence of rational restraints and of impersonalizing inhibitions; again, vitality and personality 'out of place'; including vulgarity of manners and all indiscreetly personal behavior.

We have thus arrived at the key concept of *moral* disgust, which should not be confused with moral condemnation in general—let alone, with indignation at evil deeds—nor with the condemnatory response to sexual immorality in particular, nor even with moral contempt. Meanness and cowardice are specifically contemptible; gross lying, cynical hypocrisy and sharp practice are revolting rather than disgusting; some stark and gravely reprehensible acts of lust may fail to be typically disgusting. What is eminently disgusting in a moral context, then? I would tentatively answer: the *shirókaya natura* of the Russians (prior to Bolshevism, at any rate); inconsistency and irresponsibility; what the French call *inconscience*, overspontaneity, overpersonalness, softness, and sentimentalism; above all, what the Germans call *Verlogenheit*: that is, a character organically wedded to, a mental life diffusely steeped in, lying, dissembling, illusion, and self-deception. Unlovable as the puritanical type of character may be, it forms an extreme contrast with the morally disgusting. I have come across some writers (in diverse nations) who, without being at all pornographic in the Rabelaisian or the Proustian, much less in a more vulgar, technical and meretricious sense, and being completely alien to, say, Nietzsche's titanic or Shaw's systematic immoralism, have appeared to me somehow palpably unclean and peculiarly disgusting. Would Lawrence Sterne be a good example? But then I couldn't read him. Perhaps Jean Giradoux, or some of the women novelists (but only a minority of these). Of the two best known great—by no means the greatest—German lyrical poets of the early twentieth century, Stefan George is utterly odious but not disgusting at all, whereas R.M. Rilke, who has nothing odious about him, is slightly disgusting.

It is in disgust that intention and condition form the most perfect, interpenetrating and reposeful harmony: we float in a nausea intimately adapted to the object we are intentionally—reluctantly but somehow responsively—immersed in. This contrasts with the linear and as it were accidental nexus between object and self that characterizes fear. It also contrasts with hatred which, like fear though in a very different way, is highly existential, and, even if in fact it fails to issue in outward action, is of its essence tensely directed to ruthless action upon its object as opposed to sampling and mere 'ejection'.

6. Hatred and Destruction (or Hostility, or Oppugnancy)

Prototypically, the 'movement' proper to hatred is directed to the destruction of its object; or at least to an impact on the object stopping short of destruction but aligned with it and consonant to its spirit or symbolic of destruction in one essential respect (humiliation, insult, expulsion, etc.). But, if all hatred is inspired and governed by a destructive intention, the reverse does not hold: fear (that is, the urge for self-protection), gain (the urge for pleasure, possession or creation), or more in general, the striving for advantage or amelioration, these may underlie a destructive intent without the slightest intervention of hatred. It is only destruction 'for its own sake' that is aimed at in hatred; in other words, hatred presupposes dislike, condemnation, reprobation or loathing. Further, as hinted just above, the destructive intent—even if the last-named basic postulate of intrinsic rejection and reprehension is satisfied—may be a strongly qualified and circumscribed one. We hate some human (or spiritual) entity: a person, a group of persons, even a camp or cause, without aiming at its integral annihilation or even wishing or inefficaciously desiring to so annihilate it. In a stretched and marginal sense of hatred, we may indeed hate what we consider an odious *feature*[5] in an object we do not as such hate but perhaps definitely love, and intend to purify, improve, perfect and indeed benefit by 'destroying' or 'correcting' this or that specific disvalue adhering to it. It might also be said in such a case that we do not hate the object in question but are angry at it, in a degree perhaps proportionate to our love for it. How far this is really possible is a problematic matter.[6] The fine-sounding Augustinian adage 'Hate the sin, love the sinner' is gravely misleading in as much as it suggests an utterly false analogy between 'sin' (moral disvalue, wickedness) and illness or affliction. In the latter context, of course the more we love a person, the more we hate (are eager to combat or remove) that which weakens, disables, tortures, and disfigures him, and in no way expresses him or is identifiable with him. But sin is what the sinner does; the work of his agency, which proceeds from his will and represents him, and for which he is responsible. If I say I hate the sin but love the sinner I either don't understand the words I am using or am saying at least one of the two things without meaning it seriously. In some cases, it might be held that anger is present but hatred is not (for example, in response to moral weakness or carelessness distinguishable from actual wickedness); in other cases the best phrasing would perhaps be that hatred is capable of being restrained and circumscribed, and that it ought to be subject to the mandatory moral law of justice and the hortatory law of charity. In any event, hatred (and anger) cannot be 'adjectival', that is, feature-directed, without remainder, though loathing can; it is essentially 'substantival', entity-directed, that is, directed against a person or persons (in a fashion however mediated by properties), and involves enmity (however subject to limitations and charged with provisos and counter-weights). Ambivalence (*Hassliebe*) appears to me definitely possible, howsoever difficult of analysis it may be.

This, as it were, historical character of hatred—its nascence from, or building round, a situation of 'hostile encounter'—brings in a second familiar puzzle. If hatred is not simply a hardening or an object-engulfing expansion of dislike, disapproval or condemnation, could it be (as certain popular philosophies would have it) that in reality the historical or situational factor plays the primary role? Hatred would then be a mere function of fear (the experience of being threatened) or perhaps of revenge (in response to one's having been harmed), or, putting it more cautiously and commonsensically, an outgrowth of the experience of *being thwarted* in one's design; and the agent, once having come to hate an object would then secondarily tend to 'discover'—and, partly, invent—its repulsiveness and evilness, its defects and demerits. The outlook underlying this view is that of the 'sublime' theories that all hatred originates in 'error' or in an 'undeveloped' state of the hater, and 'unclearness' of his ideas (Spinoza), closely tied up (as sublime theories are likely to be) with the crude naturalism which interprets men's attitudes of all kinds in terms of the brutish instincts (pleasure-seeking and self-assertion). Yet, in fact, hatred never is a mere reaction to personal threat or even personal affront, just as on the other hand it never is mere moral reprobation or repugnance. The dual aspect of hatred is not reducible to a monistic interpretation. It presupposes qualitative depreciation, notably moral reprobation, and also presupposes an experience of being personally and adversely affected by the existential presence (the being-a-power in the world) and demeanor of the object: a relation of hostility germinally *suggested* by the configuration of facts. The central and unifying act of hatred seems to me to be a self-imposed—or quasi-imposed and accepted—*commitment* to hostility. Hatred connotes a tinge of free will more than do fear (fright, dread) or disgust. (There is also such an ingredient of freedom in some love attitudes and even in falling or being in love, I believe, as contrasted with liking, enjoying, or being pleased.[7])

Is hatred necessarily a moral sentiment, that is, directed against what is experienced as moral evil, or rather *something* morally evil (and *Dasein*-relevant, that is, existentially obtrusive)? I dare not conjecture a definite answer in the affirmative, but feel inclined to it. Of course, not only is moral condemnation possible without hatred (for example, in what sense can we hate Nero or the Borgias?); it is also possible that the evil party in a conflict should hate his virtuous opponent, and not merely feel incommoded, frustrated and threatened by him. But this objection is to a large extent countervailed by reminding oneself that the intentional may widely differ from the real object. Hatred may well attach to a specious conception of rights and wrongs. Unbelievable as it appeared to me during 1914–18, I could not help noticing that many people in the area of the Central Powers were *bona fide* (or almost so?) convinced that *their* cause was the good and that of the Allies the evil one, though a more intelligent and more depraved minority already toyed with the more recent totalitarism sophistry which teaches that 'conventional' or 'bourgeois' morality is only Professor Hare's 'morality in inverted commas', to be resolutely done away with by more genuine 'moral decisions' of a different kind, by the divine superiority of spurting 'vital force', by the 'logic of history' or some similar tommy-rot.[8] But any abject criminal may easily come to hate the police detective or the public prosecutor as an 'infernal, interfering busybody' or perhaps as a mercenary sworn to protect 'ill-gotten gains', etc., that is, credit him with specified moral disvalue. In general, the language of hatred even as used by scoundrels tends to be a moral language (and appropriately vulgar). It is widely held that people gravely smitten with the contemptible vice of envy are apt to hate their more fortunate neighbors (and *a fortiori*, rivals) as beneficiaries of an 'injustice'. *Malicious envy*, I submit, implies indignation—however unjustified. I once expressed my difficulty in believing that a jealous lover, not *jilted* by the object of his attentions but simply turned down by a girl in favor of another aspirant, could actually hate his successful rival; but Professor Bernard Williams sternly pointed out that I must be an uncommonly rational person—too much of a rationalist, that is, to be a philosopher. I confess here to a sense of bafflement.

The intention of hatred is inquisitive, aggressive, propulsive. It impinges not only on the object as such but on its existential status in the world and thereby on the world itself, with an eye on its finiteness: the world is, as it were, 'too narrow a place to hold us both'. Not immersed in the concern with his own safety or lost in the contemplation of the repulsiveness of its object, the hater is a claimant, however ineffectual or hopeless, for participation in the shaping of the universe. This is what lends hatred its peculiar trail of tautness and concentration on the condition side—very much less susceptible of autonomous description than are the conditions, respectively, of fear and of disgust (and many others like anger, irritation, or boredom).

7. The Asymmetry or Categorical Autonomy of the Aversions

Without denying that some general descriptions could also be made of liking, loving, desiring, admiring, approving, assenting and so on, with only a minimum of reference to their objects and the manifold activities to which these attitudes are linked, and allowing on the other hand that I did have to make references to the objects of disgust (though less to those of hatred, and least to those of fear), what we may recognize is that a far higher degree of abstract typological characterization is possible on the negative or aversion side. Any project of attempting an analogous description of the modes of attraction would tempt us into describing life itself. That is so because our positive contacts, our consonances and our endeavors of union and communion with objects are functional, with their respective nature closely adapted to the manifoldness of the actual and possible objects and of the kinds of activity they invite or lend themselves to. No schema comparable to the triad of flight, repugnance (as the result of tentative tasting), and destruction (however toned down), even with the conceivable addition of a few more, similarly abstract and formal modes, could be applied to the inexhaustible world of our pro attitudes and love-like attentions. Between, say, the appetite for food and that for certain kinds of cloth or leather, the difference is immensely greater than the difference between our disgust aroused by certain smells and that aroused by certain tactile impressions; striving to 'use' a thing is a concept immeasurably more multidimensional and less linear than seeking to withdraw from its range of action; and neither friendship nor erotic union nor religious communion nor co-operation towards definite goals nor self-contained enjoyment of a person's company or existence, etc., etc., offers anything like a fitting analogon to the unequivocal meaning of suppression and opposition. Hobbes's thesis that the most important thing we can do to one another is to kill one another is incontrovertible. It may only be hoped that it is the most important *single* thing, and the most definite or rather the most definitive thing we can do to one another, but not necessarily more important in volume and significance than the illimitable variety of the benefits we can and do bestow upon our fellow creatures and receive or gently extort from them.

Afterword by David Wiggins

The above essay was written, probably in 1969–1970, for the weekly seminar of the philosophy department at Bedford College, London, where Kolnai was Lecturer in Ethics from 1959 until his death in 1973. The park mentioned in Section 1 is Regent's Park. The seminar room itself overlooked the lake. The paper was written in response to my request to Dr. Kolnai that he present to the seminar some of the ideas he had first developed in 'Der Ekel' (*Jahrhuch für Philosophie und phänomenologische Forschung* X, 1929; reprinted Tübingen: Max Niemeyer, 1974). See p. 226 of the Bibliography in *Ethics, Value, and Reality,* edited by F. Dunlop and B. Klug (London: Athlone / Indianapolis: Hackett, 1978). This book also contains a biographical sketch and philosophical appraisal of Kolnai, written by Bernard Williams and myself. The text of the present article is an edited version of the manuscript to be deposited in the Kolnai archive at King's College, London. For this manuscript see p. 237 of *Ethics, Value, and Reality.* (The Bedford College philosophy department was merged with the King's College philosophy department in one of the academic reorganizations of the early 1980s.)

The first footnote makes an autobiographical echo. Kolnai's most celebrated work, a comprehensive critique of the doctrines and political roots of German National Socialism, entitled *The War Against the West* (London: Gollancz / New York: Viking Press, 1938), was written in a Vienna café frequented by Austrian Nazis. Some related thoughts will be found in *The Utopian Mind and Other Papers*, edited by Francis Dunlop (London: Athlone, 1995).

[Kolnai's philosophical autobiography, *Political Memoirs*, was edited and abridged for publication by Francesca Murphy (Lanham: Lexington Books, 1999). Francis Dunlop has written an account of Kolnai's whole life and work, *The Life and Thought of Aurel Kolnai* (Aldershot: Ashgate, 2002).]

Notes

VISCERAL VALUES: AUREL KOLNAI ON DISGUST

1. Paul Ekman and W.V. Friesen, *Unmasking the Face: A Guide to Recognizing Emotions from Facial Expressions* (Englewood Cliffs: Prentice Hall, 1975).

2. A larger catalogue of philosophical explorations of disgust is provided in Winfried Menninghaus, 'Ekel', *Ästhetische Grundbegriffe*, Vol. 2 (Stuttgart, Weimar: Verlag J.B. Metzler, 2001), pp. 142–177.

3. This essay was written about 1969–70 but not published until 1998 in the journal *Mind*. See David Wiggins's 'Afterword' to the essay reprinted on pp. 108–09 below.

4. William Ian Miller, *The Anatomy of Disgust* (Cambridge, MA: Harvard University Press, 1997); Noël Carroll, *The Philosophy of Horror* (New York: Routledge, 1990); Cynthia Freeland, *The Naked and the Undead* (Boulder: Westview, 2000); Julia Kristeva, *The Powers of Horror*, trans. Leon S. Roudiez (New York: Columbia University Press, 1982).

5 *Psychoanalyse und Soziologie* (Vienna/Leipzig: Internationaler Psychoanalytischer Verlag, 1920). Kolnai seems to have moved away from Freud partly as a result of the influence of Scheler.

6. His conversion and aspects of his theology are presented in Chapter 4 of his posthumously published memoirs: Aurel Kolnai, *Political Memoirs*, ed. Francesca Murphy (Lanham: Lexington Books, 1999).

7. *The War Against the West* (London: Gollancz; New York: Viking, 1938). Kolnai gives an account of his experiences with National Socialism in *Political Memoirs*, especially Chapters 7, 8, and 10.

8. See Barry Smith, *Austrian Philosophy: The Legacy of Franz Brentano* (Chicago: Open Court, 1994).

9. Franz Brentano, *Psychology from an Empirical Standpoint* (1874), ed. Linda L. McAlister (New York: Humanities Press, 1973).

10. Ronald De Sousa, *The Rationality of Emotion* (Cambridge, MA: MIT Press, 1987).

11. Characteristic of Scheler's thinking is the idea of different orders or ranks of 'higher' and 'lower' value. He employed this notion *inter alia* in defense of various different forms of elitism. His eulogies of war are also eulogies of the Prussian army as an elite military institution charged with the task of defending what he saw as the higher values of German culture. His writings on religion are also eulogies of the Roman Catholic Church as an elite body which is destined to save mankind from the English calculatory spirit.

12. Different senses of 'cognitivism' in emotion theory are reviewed by John Deigh, 'Cognitivism in the Theory of Emotions', *Ethics* 104 (July, 1994), 824–854.

13. The neurologist Antonio R. Damasio, for example, argues that brain lesions that injure the portions of the prefrontal lobe not only destroy the capacity to experience certain types of emotions but also render the patient unable to function with practical knowledge in the world. (*Descartes' Error: Emotion, Reason, and the Human Brain* (New York: Grosset/Putnam, 1994).

14. *Ethics, Value, and Reality: Selected Papers of Aurel Kolnai*, Francis Dunlop and Brian Klug, eds., with an Introduction by David Wiggins and Bernard Williams (London: Athlone Press, 1977; Indianapolis: Hackett, 1978).

15. Anthony Savile, 'Sentimentality', in *The Test of Time: An Essay in Philosophical Aesthetics* (Oxford: Clarendon, 1982).

16. Some influential cognitivist theories of emotions include Ronald de Sousa, *The Rationality of Emotions,* op. cit.; Robert Gordon, *The Structure of Emotion* (Cambridge: Cambridge University Press, 1987). For a complex treatment of belief, see Patricia Greenspan on "propositional feelings," *Emotions and Reasons* (New York: Routledge, 1988).

17. De Sousa, for example, argues that there is no genus 'emotion' of which particular emotions are differentia.

18. See for example Jenefer Robinson, 'Startle', *Journal of Philosophy* XCII:2 (February, 1995), 53–75; and 'Emotion, Judgment, and Desire', *Journal of Philosophy* LXXX:11 (November, 1983), 731–741; John Morreall, 'Fear Without Belief', *Journal of Philosophy* 90:7 (July 1993), 359–366.

19. Paul Griffiths, *What Emotions Really Are: The Problem of Psychological Categories* (Chicago: University of Chicago Press, 1997). Griffiths takes the term 'affect program' from psychologist Paul Ekman.

20. Griffiths, p. 16. This does not render emotions, including affect programs, 'noncognitive', for they have crucial roles in understanding the world. See Griffiths's comments about the misleading nature of the term 'cognitive', pp. 2–3.

21. Miller, p. 36.

22. Charles Darwin, *The Expression of the Emotions in Man and Animals* (1872) (Chicago: University of Chicago Press, 1965), pp. 256–58.

23. "In evolution, disgust probably helped motivate organisms to maintain an environment sufficiently sanitary for their health and to prevent them from eating spoiled food and drinking polluted water." Carroll Izard, *Human Emotions* (New York: Plenum, 1977) p. 337.

24. Paul Rozin and April E. Fallon, 'A Perspective on Disgust', *Psychological Review* 94:1 (1987), pp. 23–41; and Paul Rozin, Jonathan Haidt, Clark R. McCauley, 'Disgust', in Michael Lewis and Jeannette M. Haviland, eds., *Handbook of Emotions* (New York: Guilford Press), pp. 575–594.

25. Nico H. Frijda, *The Emotions* (Cambridge: Cambridge University Press, 1986), p. 11.

26. See also the psychological studies reported by Rozin, Haidt, and McCauley in 'Disgust'.

27. Claire Margat, Preface to Aurel Kolnai, *Le dégoût*, trans. Olivier Cossé (Paris: Agalma, 1997), p. 6. Margat's preface situates Kolnai's essay in relation to surrealism, existentialism, and psychoanalysis. See also Robert Radford, 'Aurel Kolnai's Disgust: A Source in the Art and Writing of Salvador Dali', *The Burlington Magazine* 141:1150 (January, 1999); Rosalind Krauss, *L'Informe*, Exhibition Catalogue (Paris: Centre Pompidou, 1996).

28. Georges Bataille, *Oeuvres Complètes*, Vol. II (1922–40), (Paris: Gallimard, 1970), pp. 438–39.

29. Jean-Paul Sartre, *Nausea*, trans. Lloyd Alexander (New York: New Directions, 1964 [1938]), p. 134.

30. Miller, pp. 40–41. Compare Jacques Lacan's comment that "life is putrefaction." (Seminar XVII, *The Ethics of Psychoanalysis*).

31. Noël Carroll, Chapter 1, 'The Nature of Horror'.

32. Paul Ekman, Robert W. Levenson, and Wallace V. Friesen, 'Autonomic Nervous System Activity Distinguishes among Emotions', *Science* 221 (16th September, 1983), p. 1209.

33. Andrew J. Calder, Andrew D. Lawrence, and Andrew W. Young, 'Neuropsychology of Fear and Loathing', *Nature* (May, 2001), 352-363.

34. Kolnai returned to this claim again and again. Even in his autobiography he remarks, on a personal note, that "Our very being is empty and meaningless without love, whereas it is conceivable without hatred; love does not necessarily presuppose a corresponding hatred, whereas hatred postulates a background of things loved on whose behalf we turn against what threatens them" (*Political Memoirs*, p. 70). In an obituary from 1936 on the deaths of Karl Kraus and G.K. Chesterton, Kolnai wrote, "Let us

admit that love and hatred are, neither in the human soul nor in the scale of values, symmetrically corresponding quantities." Trans. by Istvan Selmeczi and Leslie Tihany: 'Magi of the Reasoning Mind: Karl Kraus and Gilbert Keith Chesterton', (*The Chesterton Review* XIII:3 [August, 1987], p. 311).

35. Kolnai groups these three emotions together, but there are other combinations that have been studied as well. Izard calls disgust, anger, and contempt the "hostility triad" (*Human Emotions*, p. 89); and Rozin, Haidt, and McCauley also consider these three to function together as "moral emotions."

36. Miller, Chapter 6, 'Fair is Foul and Foul is Fair'.

37. Miller, p. 200.

38. Martha Nussbaum, '"Secret Sewers of Vice": Disgust, Bodies, and the Law', in Susan Bandes, ed., *The Passions of Law* (New York: New York University Press 1999); *Upheavals of Thought: The Intelligence of Emotions* (Cambridge: Cambridge University Press, 2001), esp. section 4.

39. Kolnai wrote an entire book on sexual ethics: *Sexualethik* (Paderborn: Schöningh, 1930). An English translation is being prepared by Francis Dunlop, who is also translating Kolnai's *Der ethische Wert und die Wirklichkeit* (*Ethical Value and Reality*, 1927).

40. Winfried Menninghaus believes that Kolnai follows Karl Rosenkranz in his assessment of the sentimentality of Romantic literature ('Ekel', op. cit., p. 164). Rosenkranz's *Ästhetic des Hässlichen* (1853) is one of the works on the topic of disgust that Kolnai notes in his Concluding Bibliographical Remark. See also Menninghaus, *Ekel: Theorie und Geschichte einer starken Empfindung* (Frankfurt am Mein: Suhrkamp, 1999).

41. *Political Memoirs*, p. 5.

42. Alexius Meinong, *On Emotional Presentation* (1917), trans. Marie-Luise Schubert Kalsi (Evanston: Northwestern University Press, 1972); Max Scheler, *Der Formalismus in der Ethik_und die materiale Wertethik*, 2 vols. (Halle: Niemeyer, 1913–1916).

DISGUST

1. As the author explains in his opening remarks to Section II below, he is using the German term *Angst* to comprehend both 'anxiety' and 'fear'. In what follows we shall normally use the latter translation (EDITORS).

2. On 'dirt' as an exception see Section III.2(d) below.

3. By "intentionality" Kolnai means the degree of directedness of a given mental act or state towards objects. For a fuller explanation of the philosophical use of 'intention' and 'intentionality' as meaning: directed-

ness towards objects, see our Introduction above (EDITORS).

4. By "conditionality" Kolnai means the degree to which a given emotion affects the subject as a whole—affects the subject's total condition or state, including bodily condition (EDITORS).

5. That is, fear or anxiety has two intentional objects. It is directed both to an external object or state of affairs and to oneself (EDITORS).

6. Otto Weininger (1880–1903), author of *Geschlecht und Charakter* (*Sex and Character*).

THE STANDARD MODES OF AVERSION: FEAR, DISGUST, AND HATRED

1. Cf. the fear a fugitive may feel when soldiers not actually in search for him come into the cafe where he is sitting; or the imaginary fear that one will catch smallpox from the neighbors.

2. By "I fear the browse" Kolnai appears to mean: 'I fear having to wander amidst the ideosyncrancies of phobias' (EDITORS).

3. For instance I strongly dislike sherry and, more violently beetroot: yet even beetroot, which I couldn't even contrive to eat, fails to arouse disgust in me.

4. AUTHOR'S MARGINAL NOTE: "Tactile disgust: slimy softness, etc.; but its disgust-engendering power may fail completely."

5. What *is* a feature? For example, a big nose on somebody's face?

6. AUTHOR'S MARGINAL NOTE: "anger at careless cat; hatred directed against some careless driver".

7. AUTHOR'S MARGINAL NOTE: "But surplus of freedom—of the volitive element—on the side of hatred."

8. AUTHOR'S MARGINAL NOTE: "Second World War; difficult to forge moral pretence: scarce hatred on the German side."

Index

Kraus, Karl, 113n24
Krauss, Rosalind, 113n27
Kristeva, Julia, 3, 16, 17, 18,
  111n4
Külpe, Oswald, 90

Lacan, Jacques, 113n30
Lawrence, Andrew D., 113n33
Levenson, Robert W., 113n32
Lewis, Michael, 113n24
life, surplus of, 72–74
loathsome, the, 34
logical positivism, 10
love, 93, 113n34

Mann, Thomas, 67
Margat, Claire, 113n27
Marx, Karl H., 4
McAlister, Linda L., 111n9
McCauley, Clark R., 113n24,
  113n26, 114n35
Meinong, Alexius, 3, 5, 8, 25, 94,
  114n42
Menninghaus, Winfried, 111n2,
  114n40
Miller, William Ian, 3, 14, 17–18,
  21, 23, 24, 111n4, 113n21,
  113n30, 114n36, 114n37
Mises, Ludwig von, 4
Moore, George Edward, 4
Morreall, John, 112n18
Murphy, Francesca, 111n6

nausea, 34–35, 103
Nietzsche, Friedrich, 103
Nussbaum, Martha, 2, 23–24, 25,
  114n38

objects of moral disgust, 87, 103

excessive vitality, 65–68
  falsehood, 69–71
  incest, 64
  lies, 68–69
  monotony, 63–65
  moral softness, 71–72
  satiety, 63–64
objects of physical disgust, 16–22,
  30, 43–44, 47, 87, 101–02
  animals, 56–58
  dirt, 55–56, 114n2
  disease, 62
  exaggerated fertility, 61–62
  excrement, 54
  food, 59–60
  human body, the, 61
  putrefaction, 53–54
  secretions, 54
Ortega y Gasset, ix

Pascal, Blaise, 7
Pfänder, Alexander, 6, 7
phenomenology, 3, 29–30
  Munich school of, 4, 6–7
Political Memoirs, 111n6, 111n7,
  113n34, 114n41
Psychoanalysis and Sociology, 3,
  111n5
psychoanalysis, 3, 21, 42–43,
  113n27
putrefaction, moral, 84–85

Radford, Robert, 113n27
Reinach, Adolf, 6, 7
Rilke, Rainer Maria, 103
Robinson, Jenefer, 112n18
Roosevelt, Franklin D., 99
Rosenkranz, Karl, 91, 114n40
Roudiez, Leon S., 111n4
Rozin, Paul, 14–15, 16, 113n24,
  113n26, 114n35